THE TRUTH WILL SET YOU FREE

ALAN ROBINSON

The Truth Will Set You Free

ST PAULS

ST PAULS Publishing
187 Battersea Bridge Road, London SW11 3AS, UK
www.stpauls.ie

Copyright © ST PAULS 2004

ISBN 085439 684 5

Set by TuKan DTP, Fareham, Hampshire, UK
Printed by Interprint Ltd, Marsa, Malta

ST PAULS is an activity of the priests and brothers of the Society of St Paul who proclaim the Gospel through the media of social communication

CONTENTS

Introduction 7
Part I
Tapping on the shell 9

Chapter One	I can't believe in God?	11
Chapter Two	What's in it for me?	31
Chapter Three	What is God like anyway?	41

Part II
God's self-portrait 57

Chapter Four	Father figure	59
Chapter Five	Everybody's brother	69
Chapter Six	The ghost in the machine	79
Chapter Seven	Threefold mystery	89

Part III
History is more than a book 97

Chapter Eight	Just a few words	99
Chapter Nine	With foresight	107
Chapter Ten	Old sinners and new saints	117
Chapter Eleven	Unbroken chain	141
Chapter Twelve	The end of all things	149

Part IV
Year in, year out 157

Chapter Thirteen	Alone with eternity	159
Chapter Fourteen	Singing the faith	171
Chapter Fifteen	Map reading	181

Introduction

Many people find at one stage in their lives that they are imprisoned in a symbolic sense by some controlling force. This may be caused by selfishness, or by bad habits, or by apathy, or by any number of human failings. Sometimes life is so busy that it is not easy to escape from such a prison, which may be preventing people from living their lives to the full. Love may become stunted, and talents may be denied the opportunity to grow.

It is good now and again for all of us to take a little time to consider where we are going, where our lives are leading us. However, not everyone has sufficient time to spare to think about the serious options which may help to plan the life ahead. This book tries to consider one such option in a brief space so that even the busiest person, given a little effort, will be able to find time to read what is presented, which is the "God option" offered by Christianity.

The very mention of God may bring negative images and feelings to the front of some people's minds. Moreover, all the arguments against the possible existence of God may come to the surface, and to be sure, some of the arguments appear at first sight to be strong ones. However, the very first chapter of the book considers the main "against-God" arguments and gives a strong and convincing case for believing in the Christian God. The book then outlines the many advantages of becoming a

Christian and goes on to give a detailed description of the character of God as revealed in the Bible and through the Church.

In later chapters the Christian perspective in relation to the history of the world is considered. Also, a brief outline of the unbroken chain of the Christian revelation is given, with mention of some of the great figures in the continuing tradition of four thousand years. The book concludes with a discussion of practical Christianity in relation to everyday life, considering for example, prayer, worship and moral guidelines.

The book will be useful not only for non-Christians who wish to explore the basic ideas behind Christian faith and belief, but will also be helpful to Christians who wish to rediscover their faith.

I
Tapping on the shell

Just as a bird taps on the shell before it emerges, so we may tap on the shell of our own little world in order to emerge into a greater reality. This section considers the arguments against God's existence and gives a range of Christian answers to these problems. Further, the advantages of becoming a Christian are briefly considered in relation to our every day lives. Then a preliminary look is taken at what sort of being God might be. This sets the scene for a more detailed look at the Christian God in Part II of the book.

CHAPTER ONE

I can't believe in God

This chapter considers ten reasons that people often give for not believing in God, together with a Christian response in each case.

1. Why is there so much suffering in the world?

Why, if God exists, does he allow so many nasty and painful things to happen in the world? The evidence of pain and suffering is there, of course, and it is not easy to explain it, if you believe in a good and loving God. In fact, many clever people over many centuries have tried to solve this problem, but without a lot of success. Why did three thousand people die in that earthquake? Surely God could have made a better job of making this planet. Why are children dying of hunger in some parts of Africa? Surely God could provide food when probably a lot of the hungry people have prayed for some, perhaps even using Jesus' prayer (*Give us this day our daily bread*). Why are people so cruel? Surely God could have made people so that they would be kind to each other. All in all, if somebody did create the universe, he can't be very good at creating.

Way back before the time of Jesus, clever people had identified this problem. One Greek philosopher put it something like this. *If God is perfectly good he must wish to end evil in the world. If he is all-powerful he can do whatever he wishes. So why doesn't he act to put an end to all the evils we experience?*

Of course, it could be argued that some of the suffering in the world is caused by people not by God. On the other hand some suffering is caused by natural disasters, which in insurance terms have often been called acts of God. It is clear then, that there are at least two kinds of evil. The suffering caused by wicked people may be described as moral evil, whereas the suffering caused by natural disasters may be called natural evil. Both of these need some sort of explanation by those who believe in God.

Response

It is true that the existence of evil in the world is difficult to accept, and it is not easy for Christians to explain why God has brought such a world into existence. However, Christians believe that Christ was God's Son and that God himself in Christ came into the world to become one with us and to suffer with us and for us. That, of course, cannot be proved immediately, though it is capable of proof in the ultimate. The trouble is we have to wait until we're dead to find such proof.

If a loving God exists and if he did create a world where suffering is inevitable, then he must have had good reasons for doing so. One possible reason is that a world without suffering would not allow people to develop the character or the soul (essential part of being), ready for further development in another dimension. If people lived in a luxurious paradise where no effort was necessary, then they would be just like vegetables.

The suffering caused by people may be explained more readily than suffering caused by natural disasters. After all, if God gives people personal responsibility, he must allow for bad and even evil, decision-making. The natural disaster on the other hand, seems to have little value, except that the people who help those who suffer are bringing much good into the situation and into the world. Challenges of all kinds bring out the best in people. Even so, it has to be admitted that some aspects of suffering remain a mystery, even to the most perceptive Christian.

Those who believe in God have to recognise that some mysteries will not be resolved in this life. If, however, a person's faith is strong, then he will trust the good and loving God in any of life's situations. Injustice and suffering may exist in the here and now, but in the end God will set all things right. If God does exist, this must be so.

The situation of children in school provides a convincing parallel to the position of every human being as he goes through life. The value of an education is often not appreciated until school is far behind. Similarly, the value of life experiences may not be appreciated until this life has ended and new life brings understanding.

2. There is no evidence

Some people argue that there is no evidence that God exists. Over the centuries, philosophers have come up with some very clever arguments to try to prove the existence of God, but their efforts are not completely convincing. The believer may point to the intricacies and the beauty of the universe and claim that God must have created it, but the sceptic may simply say that the universe has always been there, along with the evolutionary process, and no creator is needed to bring things into existence. In another similar argument, the believer may contend that God must have been the First Cause that started off the universe, but the sceptic may argue that there is no need for a First Cause because there never was a beginning. The believer may point to all the wonderful people there have been in the history of all of the great religions, but the sceptic may argue that such people are deluded, or that they are serving society's best interests, and not some imaginary God's will. For all the arguments in favour of God existing, there seem to be counter arguments. If the evidence were to be presented in a court of law what would a judge conclude? Would he say the evidence points towards the existence of God, or not?

Other people put a similar argument about evidence in a rather different way. They say they only accept the existence of things they can experience through the senses. From this position they argue that ideas like *God* and *heaven* have no real existence because they cannot be experienced through any of the five senses. Ideas connected with God are confined to the human imagination. Of course, by the same token, neither can the devil have any real existence. The idea of Satan is simply a way of classifying human behaviour. Similarly, God is merely a human construct designed to persuade people to behave according to certain social rules.

Response

Scientific proof is not an appropriate way to find evidence for God's existence. To take a parallel example, it is not necessary to prove that beauty exists. This is because there is an immediate awareness of beauty when certain experiences "arrive" through the senses. A sunset or the song of a blackbird is perceived as beautiful without any proof being necessary. In any case, it is notoriously difficult to define beauty. Love falls into the same category. The mother needs no proof that she loves her child or that this love is returned. Similarly, religious awareness provides its own proof. This is a strong inner feeling that an almighty but good personal power is close. Some of the words which have been used to describe this sense of God's presence are *holy, majestic* and *otherworldly*.

How may this God-awareness be brought to mind? Well, of course, sometimes the experience comes unexpectedly. However, in some circumstances there is a predisposition in the mind towards such an experience. For example, if a person sat on a mountain-top on a clear night to watch the stars, he might be overcome by a sense of an almighty power behind what we call normal reality. Yet again, if a person ventured into a really ancient and beautiful cathedral, he might be overcome by a sense of a holy presence without being able to explain it.

Other types of experience may convince someone that God lies behind and through what we call reality. For example, if a person was almost killed in some kind of accident or natural catastrophe, then he might be convinced that a divine being had stepped in to save him. Similarly, if a person had a serious illness and was close to death, though by some miracle making a good recovery, he might be filled with awe by the nature of his experience.

One difference between this kind of conviction from experience and scientific proof is that it may not be possible to convince another person of God's existence on this basis. However, sometimes people have shared an awesome experience, in which case they could share a conviction that God was somehow making himself known through that common experience.

Special experiences, then, may lead to religious conviction, and such evidence may be compelling enough to change a person's whole perspective. However, an individual needs to have the experience himself before being convinced of its validity in providing for him proof of God's existence. This, of course, can be true of natural phenomena. For example, if one man says he has actually seen a blue moon, even his closest friends may not believe him; but if he can take them to see the blue moon, then they will be convinced.[1]

In the Bible there is a story of how three disciples went with Jesus to the top of a mountain. There they saw Jesus transfigured into a heavenly vision in which he was with two other beings.[2] Later in the Gospel story some disciples had an experience of the risen Jesus. These people did not require evidence of God's existence. Their own personal experience was proof enough.[3]

3. When people die that is the end

Our fore knowledge of death is a strong argument against any existence beyond this life. Death is so final. When we die, our bodies return to their basic elements by one process or another. As far as the observer is concerned, the dead person no longer exists except as a memory. If, then, there is no after life, the idea of a personal God who created us recedes into the realm of improbability.

The word *improbability* is chosen carefully. It is not at all the same as *impossibility*. In fact, while there are several quite convincing arguments against the existence of God, it is difficult to prove that God does not exist. That is why many people prefer to call themselves agnostics, rather than atheists.

Response

The Christian claim that life continues after death is mainly based on the resurrection of Jesus and the biblical promises that go along with it. The difficulty with that for the present day seeker after truth is that all the alleged witnesses of the resurrection are themselves long since dead. Of course, it is possible to believe in life after death without being a Christian. Other higher religions hold to a similar belief. However, this response is mainly from the Christian viewpoint, though more general arguments may be used as well.

Life is full of question marks, some of them related to the meaning of life, if life indeed has a meaning. If a person lives for seventy-five years, he may towards the end feel that the meaning of his life is not yet fulfilled. It may be that he is aware of a need for a final explanation of his reason for being. The very fact that the question is there implies a logical necessity for completion. Such completion is only possible if life continues beyond the crematorium.

Many near to death experiences are recorded. In some of these the body seems to be lifeless, but when the person "returns" he reports that he has come to the edge of another life in some way. Some people claim to have seen their own "dead" bodies while having a "post-death" experience. In addition, many people who die and do not return seem convinced at the moment of death that they are approaching some form of renewal in another life. Some witnesses, who have often been close to dying people in a professional capacity, claim that a great number of dying people seem convinced they are going on to something else.

Some Christians, in addition to the original witnesses, claim to have had experience of the risen Jesus. Certainly this is what St Paul claimed, though of course he was contemporary with many of the first witnesses to the resurrection. However, while it may be rare for people today to claim to have had a vision of Christ, many are nevertheless convinced that he has been close to them in spirit, possibly at a time of prayer, or even while going about their daily affairs. Other people feel the presence of the risen Christ in a very special way while taking the sacrament of communion.

It may be difficult to prove conclusively that the Christian claim for the "resurrection of the body" is true. Nevertheless, some Christians have a very strong conviction that Christ rose from the dead. Historically some people have accepted martyrdom rather than recant their faith in Christ because they believed they would be resurrected with him. On the whole, however, belief in the resurrection is a matter of appraisal and judgement of a range of evidence. This evidence includes the Gospel stories about the resurrection appearances of Jesus. As might be expected, some contradictions in the stories exist, but on the whole accounts are very compelling.

There are some interesting parables in nature which seem to point to new life after an apparent death. A caterpillar appears to die and is then resurrected in a very beautiful form as a butterfly. Day follows night with a new awakening. Spring follows winter with a new arousal of nature. This is poetry and poetry tells its own truth, just as religion does.

A different kind of parable goes some way towards explaining how God recreates people in a resurrection. Many people use computers and they save material on floppy disks. If the floppy disk is destroyed they can still find the material on the hard disk of the computer. If God is represented by the computer and the mind (or soul) of a human being is represented by a floppy disk, then when the person dies, God still has all the information about that person. Just as a computer user can then put the material onto another floppy disk, so God can put his record of a particular human being into another body, and in another dimension. Like all analogies this one has its limitations, but it does try to make an important point.

4. I can't believe in miracles or visions

Some people are turned off Christianity by the miraculous elements which are claimed to accompany faith in God. Many miracles are recorded in the Bible and the sceptic may dismiss the idea of a virgin birth, or of turning water into wine, or of Jesus calming a storm or raising a person from death (as in the story about Lazarus). Alongside doubt about miracles, sceptics find it difficult to believe that God communicates with people through visions, dreams or in other ways. Of course stories about miracles and divine communications are not confined to the Bible. Over the Christian centuries many people have claimed to have experience of such supernatural events. However, non-believers throw cold water on any claim that supernatural events can happen.

Response

There are, of course, many miracles in nature, though by definition these are not supernatural. The point is, though, some natural happenings are so wonderful that to describe them as "miraculous" seems appropriate. To quote but a few examples: there is the capacity of the skin to heal itself; there is the growth of living creatures from eggs and the development of plants from seeds; and there is the almost unimaginable magnificence of the universe. People already live in the sphere of the miraculous, though they are so used to it that they do not notice. The miracles described in the Bible are no more wonderful than the miracles of nature. If God created this complicated universe, would it not be a simple matter for him to allow what are called supernatural miracles in some circumstances?

People who perform miracles may be using powers which are always there for those who have the special gift needed to use them. As human knowledge increases, it may become apparent that what are regarded as supernatural happenings may, in fact, be within the scope of higher laws of nature which the world does not yet fully understand. Suppose, for example, a man claimed that he had discovered a process by which people could place their laundry in a box for one minute and that it would emerge washed, dried and ironed. This would seem to be impossible, but if a man in the thirteenth century had claimed he had two boxes, one to wash clothes in an hour, and the other to dry clothes in an hour, that would then have seemed impossible. Yet that is precisely what happens today in washing machines and tumble dryers. In the future, then, all kinds of miracles may be possible as human knowledge grows.

If Jesus was the Son of God, then it would not be surprising if he had the power to perform miracles. Most of the miracles of Jesus were performed to help people or to give signs of his Messiah-ship. He did not, however, set out to fulfil his vocation as Messiah by being a miracle worker. The story of his temptation shows that he decided not to shock the world into godly faith through his divine power.[4] Instead he chose to be a suffering servant. His infrequent and caring use of miracles supports a convincing argument for believing the Gospel stories. If they were fictional, then the miraculous element would have been emphasised much more.

While it is true that faith is a key factor in whether or not people accept the miraculous in the Gospel stories, even so it has been shown that there are several important supporting arguments, as described above.

5. Different religions make contradictory claims

One difficulty for some people is that various religions claim that their sacred books have been revealed by God, and yet the books of different religions contradict each other. This is true, for example, of the Christian Bible and the Koran. One of the main differences between the two books is acceptance or non-acceptance that Jesus was the Son of God. In the Koran Jesus is taken to be a prophet, whereas in the Bible Jesus is regarded as divine. In Christianity this idea developed into the doctrine of the Trinity which claims that God is three persons, Father, Son and Holy Spirit. For Muslims, however, such a belief is impossible because they believe it contradicts the Oneness of God. So, the sceptic argues: how can both religions claim that revelation of God's truth is the foundation of their faith?

Response

From the Christian viewpoint it is readily acceptable that other faiths have some true insights into the nature of God and, in fact, in some aspects of belief there is agreement among the great religious faiths. For example, the major religions would accept that there is an Almighty Creator, a Supreme Being who has ultimate control over all things. Further, the moral stances of the major faiths are quite similar. For instance, the Jewish Ten Commandments are accepted by Christians, and these moral rules are similar to those propounded by Islam and Buddhism. It is much better to emphasise the areas of agreement rather than the causes of difference. Even so, Christians believe their religion is revealed from God and there are occasions when some doctrines have to be upheld against the doctrines of other faiths. Yet, only God himself knows the complete truth and it is possible that an aspect of faith may have been misunderstood by fallible human beings. This is true of all the faiths.

The Christian, then, accepts articles of belief such as those in the Apostles' Creed[5], and is willing to defend them. However, it is wise to recognise that God exists over and beyond all human formulations, even if these are believed to have been revealed by him.

6. I can't believe that people are called personally by God

Related to the idea of revelation is the conviction that some people have that God has called them to do some particular work, possibly as a preacher, or a prophet, or a teacher, or a missionary. The sceptic, of course, will probably admit that people claiming to have such vocations may be sincere, but that they are misguided. They are doing what they want to do because of some inner motivation which has nothing to do with a supposed God.

Response

Some Christians believe that a Christian calling is a matter of inner conviction guided by an assessment of their situation. For example, they may see a need for service within the Church and feel they have the ability to perform that service. Their calling is confirmed for them by the conviction that they are doing God's work, as well as by their feeling of fulfilment.

Other Christians, however, believe their call by God is more personal. It is not often the case that such people claim to have had a Damascus Road type of experience.[6] However, special experiences are common enough, though not necessarily as dramatic as that of St Paul. To give an example, a person might notice a number of coincidental events which seem to point strongly to a particular vocation. One such coincidence is counter-signed by another, and so on, until he is convinced he has received God's call. If such "coincidences" involve meaningful texts, then the experience is even more convincing. In this context, examples of often-quoted texts are:

1. *And I heard the voice of the Lord saying, "Whom shall I send, and who will go for us?" Then I said, "Here am I? Send me."*[7]
2. *You did not choose me, but I chose you and appointed you that you should go and bear fruit and that your fruit should abide...*[8]

Other people in the Bible, apart from St Paul, record very special call experiences. Moses, for example, saw a bush in flames, though not burning away while he was near Mount Sinai. At the same time he had a strong sense of the holiness of God in that place and then he heard God's voice[9].

Such calls are very personal and have a great impact on the person concerned. However, call experiences lose something in the telling. It is not quite the same to hear about a call experience as it is to *know* you have had one.

While a call is matter of personal conviction, so many people over the Christian centuries, up to the present time, have claimed to have a call, that it is difficult for any unbiased person to dismiss the truth of such accounts.

7. Religion is unnecessary in a system of morals

All the higher religions, including Christianity, have developed moral codes, and there is remarkable agreement among them, for example, that loving and caring for other people is important. However, the non-believer will argue that a moral system does not need religious faith or revelation to authenticate it. The humanist, for example, may build up a moral system on the basis that the moral goodness is what is best for the greatest number of people. In the past, this idea has been expanded into a system which is described as *utilitarianism*, in other words, what is useful to the majority of individuals in a society. God is not needed, they say, to produce a system of ethics.

Response

The trouble with humanist ethics is that any such system is based on the opinions of fallible people. Furthermore, such systems are relative to changing circumstances. This could lead to injustice for a minority of people. To take an extreme example, it might be decided that the happiness of the greatest number of people would be served if all criminals were executed, which would not give any opportunity for appeals by the wrongly accused. In addition, for most of the offenders such a harsh punishment would be undeserved. Yet again, a humanist might argue that as most people in a state are prosperous and well fed, then the minority who are poor should be ignored. It is true, of course, that an element of compassion does appear in many humanist systems of ethics, but by and large such concepts of love are borrowed from religious systems. For instance, the ethic of loving one's neighbour is based on Christian precedents.

By contrast, a system of ethics which is based on divine revelation has an eternal perspective. Basic rules will always remain the same. Anyone who deliberately breaks the rules is acting against God's revealed will. It is true that a woman who steals to feed her hungry children is acting against one of the rules, but her action is understandable. In fact, her act is one of love, which is the highest rule in the hierarchy of rules. This is where Christian ethics can be very flexible, yet true to its ideals. Moreover, forgiveness is part of some religious ethical systems, as for example in Christianity. When the rules are broken the person who feels guilty may turn to God and find forgiveness and peace.

Yet, a system of ethics without religion is to be respected. There are many caring and loving people who do not believe in God. However, an important question is where did these attitudes originate? Are they transferred from one of the religious systems? Or are they the result of an impulse towards the highest ideals a person can imagine? If the latter, the humanist is becoming very close to the religious person in his outlook.

Another interesting question is the reason for the appearance of morality in human experience. Why are people moral at all? Even in the case of humanist ethics there seems to be some ultimate purpose in the growth of moral systems. This in turn leads to the question as to what lies at the end of the line. Is it God or blind fate? The existence of God surely makes more sense than nothingness.

8. Promises of justice in a future life don't make sense

The non-believer may be very sceptical about what is often called *pie in the sky*, that is about promises of good things in a future life, even if people have suffered much in this life. Another aspect of this is that good behaviour will be rewarded in the next life – pie in the sky again. This is connected with the idea of punishment in the next life for the wrongdoings of this life. The concepts of heaven and hell are part of this supposed set up, and the non-believer will throw these concepts out as unnecessary and even unhelpful to ordinary people trying to live their lives happily despite their difficulties. The sceptic may go on to argue that heaven and hell are myths, just as many Bible stories are mythical. Such myths have been invented, it is claimed, to explain aspects of our experience.

Response

This life is a course of development towards an end and, as has already been mentioned, the apparently incomplete end leaves a question mark. If, however, the process of this life is a learning curve, and if that learning continues in another existence after death, then people will receive what they deserve during the new life. Justice will be done and will be seen to be done. Lessons which have not been learnt will surely have to be approached again in some way.

Ideas about heaven and hell are attempts to explain the further learning process which presumably continues after death. The picture of hell in the Bible is a frightening one, though the details of what hell might be like are a mystery. Certainly Jesus speaks of hell as a place of eternal damnation, using the word *gehenna* in his Sermon on the Mount. Jesus says that even if people say to someone, "You fool!" they will be liable to go to a place of hell-fire (Matthew 5:22). Of course, this statement has to be seen in the context of a forgiving God. Even so, the idea of hell is central to Christian belief. This means that our misdemeanours in this life are punishable in the next life. On the other hand, heaven is described as the destiny of those who turn to Christ and repent of their sins. This implies eternal life at peace with God.

What happens after death is a matter for inference. Logic and necessity appear to infer that wrongs must be righted and that some form of assessment is necessary for each soul. The word *soul* is used here to represent that part of a person, that concentration of being, which survives death. The detail of what happens is misty. However, there are many wonders in this life, so how much more wondrous must the next life be.

9. Modern scientific views contradict religious views

Sociology, of course, studies human societies systematically. Religion is sometimes regarded as the product of forces, which either by accident or design control societies. Further, psychologists study the individual and his motives, and so human behaviour may be explained in terms of psychological forces which are claimed to be irresistible, implying that sin can be explained away, that people are not responsible for their actions. Further, science as a whole, keeps changing people's views of the world. The views of the Bible and, indeed, of the sacred books of other ancient religions, are completely different from those of today. The biblical story of creation, for example, is often dismissed as scientifically inaccurate. Such changes in perspective certainly create difficulties for religious belief.

Response

Science as a whole tends to support belief in a Supreme Being. Of course, not all scientists believe in God, though quite a number do. However, for the average person, it is more a case of trying to see the world as science interprets it and then being stunned by the miracles which scientists have perceived. Such miracles are described by some scientists as natural phenomena, but these same scientists may ignore the ultimate *why* question, while acknowledging the immediate what and how questions. No doubt the moon can be described in great detail using a whole battery of scientific concepts. But science has not succeeding in explaining why the moon is so beautiful or why in certain company it can have a mysterious or romantic aura.

As to the scientific view of the world, what scientists

tell people is, of course, invaluable. However, while human perspectives may change, the eternal questions do not change. For example, the writers who described creation in the early chapters of Genesis in the Jewish Scriptures had what we would think was a limited view of the universe. Yet, their vision of a divine Creator who at his word brought the universe into being is unsurpassed. Spiritual truth and the inspirational road to understanding the world are still needed to explain the reality behind natural phenomena.

In a similar way, sociologists use their science to describe and give limited explanations of people's surface behaviour, while ignoring or bypassing the deep inner dimensions of fellowship in groups. Psychologists may probe more deeply at the individual level, giving complicated explanations to clarify the actions of an individual. However, some mysteries within the human psyche are beyond explanation, just as aspects of music, poetry and art are inexplicable.

All in all, science is wonderful, but the growing pool of scientific knowledge granted to the human race merely serves to enlarge the scope of the unknown. The larger the pool, the greater the unexplored territories which lie around its edge. The quest for scientific explanations is never ending. It is only in a vision given by God that any ultimate explanations can be formulated.

10. Religious belief does not accord with my personal experience

Personal experience is one of the most critical factors in deciding whether or not to believe in God. If people say, "Religion doesn't work for me," or "The special experience that religious people claim hasn't happened to me," then their scepticism may be difficult to overcome. Similarly, if people pray sincerely and appear to receive no response, they may well conclude that prayer is a waste of time.

Response

It is the quality of faith which is most convincing in religious experience. Even Jesus of Nazareth could do few miracles in his hometown because faith was lacking.[10] However, it would be too facile to say that it is lack of faith which prevents people from believing in God. What can be claimed is that persistence in prayer brings results. Furthermore, prayers are given various answers. The answer may be evident in what happens soon after the prayer. Or the answer may become evident in what happens much later. Or it is possible that God's answer to a request is no. For those seeking God, the best advice is to try praying and to keep on praying, but don't ask for the moon, and don't expect your sick grandmother to leap out of bed the instant you pray. Another point is that God sometimes answers prayers in unexpected ways. A prayer for funds to install a new organ in a church may seem to have been unsuccessful. Then a year later, quite unexpectedly, the church receives a large legacy from a former church member who had immigrated to Canada thirty years before.

    Prayer is the key to faith, and faith is the key to religious conviction. If a person tries to pray as sincerely as possible once a day for six months it would be surprising if there was no kind of answer. For such a trial of faith the prayers would need to be chosen very carefully. For example, it would be legitimate to ask God for help in one's daily life, or for a measure of inner peace, or for the welfare of a sick relative. It would be unwise to pray for any selfish purpose or for the doom of one's enemies. The next stage would be to try to build up a deeper relationship with God. An attempt to understand what worship means together with an effort to become more involved in worship would be good steps to take. Again, it would be surprising if there were no positive results after another six months of searching.

NOTES

1. The phrase once in a blue moon is common enough, but the present author did not believe such a phenomenon occurred until he actually saw one, though he has never seen another one since.
2. See Matthew, chapter seventeen, verses 1-13.
3. See particularly the story of Doubting Thomas in John's Gospel at chapter twenty, verses 24-29.
4. See Matthew, chapter four, verses 1-11.
5. Christian beliefs, including those of the Apostles' Creed, are examined in subsequent chapters of this book.
6. See Acts of the Apostles, chapter nine, verses 1-30.
7. See Isaiah, chapter six, verses 8-9.
8. See John, chapter fifteen, verse 16.
9. See Exodus, chapter three, verses 1-6.
10. See Mark, chapter six, verses 5-6

CHAPTER TWO

What's in it for me?

This is a fair question. What does religion offer to anyone who is exploring the possibility of becoming a Christian? Here are ten advantages in being a follower of Christ.

1. An explanation of life's purpose

Since men first began to think, they have been wondering about the meaning of life. They have asked such questions as, "Why am I here?" or "Is there not more to life than scratching for my daily bread?" Of course, various religions and philosophies have offered answers to these questions over the centuries, so what is so special about Christianity? A series of short answers may be given: God has made you for a purpose; God is watching over you and loving you; God is helping you to grow; God has a place waiting for you when this life is done. This means that from the day someone is born and possibly before, there is a blueprint for each person's development. However, people make mistakes and may become slightly warped, or even badly warped, turning away from their intended path through life. Nevertheless, the promise of Christ is that everyone can be put back onto their destined course, even if it has to be in the next dimension of life. Eventually, when we complete our journey, a wonderful and happy life awaits. This new life of the resurrection will not be a static one. There will be all sorts of vibrant experiences to enjoy. It is true that there is mystery beyond the door of death, but Christianity offers the promise of God's Son that it leads to the ultimate reality.

2. Help and strength for every day

There are times when life may be difficult. Situations at work may be awkward. Family quarrels may be a cause for worry. A person's health may be deteriorating. Trying to stretch the budget may be causing some headaches. The average person does have bad hair day now and again; and some people have to put up with constant problems which go on for months or years. On the other hand, of course, there are happy times for most people. However, whether life at any one time is a happy experience or a miserable one, there is a never failing supply of strength in the spirit, if a person is willing to tap into it. A simple prayer at any time during the day, along with a regular prayer time, can be very helpful. A regular prayer time need not be complicated. Nor need it last too long. The emergency prayer during the day can be very simple, a key word or sentence that indicates a cry for help. The power that lies behind the everyday reality of our lives, that is God himself, is always ready to help. Very many people can testify to this.

As a person grows deeper roots into the faith, his prayer life may well develop. Some thoughts on this subject are given later in this book.

3. A way to deal with guilt

Few people go through life without some regrets about hurtful things they may have done. Guilt can eat away inside a person and do a great deal of psychological damage. If someone has a lively conscience, guilt can be extremely painful, even over small matters. To heal such feelings of guilt Christianity places a great emphasis on forgiveness. This not a slot machine. There are conditions. If someone feels sincerely sorry for something he has done, then praying privately about it certainly helps. In some churches verbal confession to a priest is the norm. Either way, speaking to God is the start of reconciliation. If possible, making amends in some way to the person hurt, if that is achievable, is an important step to take. In addition, some church people find it helpful to have either a self imposed penance, or one advised by a priest. This helps the healing process. Love is at the heart of forgiveness, that is to say, love from God to the person feeling guilty, and love from the guilty person to the one hurt. There is also a need for humility. God's forgiveness is an act of grace on his part, and the guilty person needs to accept that grace. It is a serious fault of pride to nurture guilt for past actions when God has offered to forgive.

The whole idea of forgiveness is central to Christianity. The prayer that Jesus taught includes these words: *Forgive us our trespasses as we forgive those who trespass against us.* The purpose of the Passion of Christ is very much related to God's forgiveness. This, however, is a complex subject and will be discussed later in this book.

4. A moral compass

Over many centuries the moral standards of Christianity have been constant, despite the tides and currents of any particular period of history. The same is true geographically. Christian moral standards have followed the Church into every corner of the world and those standards are unchanging, whatever regime may be in power in any one country. It is true that some people have tried to twist those standards, but in vain. It is also true that other moral standards may prevail in any given society. However, for those who accept Christianity as their faith, the moral compass is unfailing. Of course, there are difficulties sometimes in interpreting the Christian moral code in particular situations. Life is not always simple. Even so, the standards are there, and those who pray for guidance will find a way through difficult decisions. The summary of the Law by Jesus[1] and the Ten Commandments[2] are at the centre of Christian morality.

5. A knowledge of God in human terms

God is limitless and eternal and it is difficult to imagine his power and majesty. However, that same God decided to explain himself to us in a way that we can all understand. God came to us, and still comes to us, in the Person of Jesus. The Jesus pictured in the four Gospels is very human. For example, before his short ministry began, he was tempted to follow the way of power in the world, but decided instead to pursue his calling as a suffering servant[3]. Yet again, before the crucifixion he was in great anguish at what lay before him, and he prayed earnestly to the Father to take such a bitter cup away from him[4]. However, he faced up to the challenge and changed the world. The Gospel picture shows that Jesus was compassionate, loving, humorous, deeply thoughtful, but yet demanding to those who wished to follow him. This same Jesus is the One people follow today. Yes, he is very demanding, but he cares for those who turn to him and offers them his undying love. The Jesus who lived two thousand years ago was God in human form, or God Incarnate. He is the third Person of the Trinity, for this is the way God has revealed himself. The place of Jesus Christ in the Godhead is discussed in later chapters of this book.

6. The joy of living

It may be argued that a person can enjoy life without being a Christian. This is perfectly true, within limits. If you have health and strength, some good friends, a reasonable amount of money and interesting things to do, you may well be happy on the surface. However, you may also feel dissatisfied with your life at a deeper level, especially if you feel you don't really know where you are going. Furthermore, if things start to go wrong in your life you may become very unhappy with no one to turn to. If you believe in Christ, then it is still good to have the advantages already mentioned, but you will find that a deeply spiritual experience will enrich your life. Also, if you find yourself in difficulties, you have a never-failing friend to turn to. God never lets people down, though he may sometimes teach them a sharp lesson. Through faith a deep spiritual happiness can grow within you, whatever the circumstances of your life.

Once you are living on the spiritual level, then you will find great fulfilment in helping and loving other people. You will find that you have skills or talents that can be developed with the Lord's help and guidance. You will look at the world with new eyes, and especially you will marvel and wonder at the miracles of creation. Within this growing relationship with God there comes also a sense of worship. This is a special way of speaking to God and of being in fellowship with him. Worship, of course, may be private or public, and both aspects provide joyful experiences. What, though, is at the heart of worship? This is a many splendoured jewel, but two aspects are particularly important, love and reverence. Love for our Creator and Preserver, and stemming from that, love for other people, infuse the whole of being. Reverence is an awareness of the might and majesty of

God who is also the one who comes to us in humility in the guise of a Servant. Worship is an answer to God's invitation to us to be at one with him in all that we do.

7. Fellowship

Fellowship is rather different from friendship, though the two are closely related. Within a fellowship there should be a combination of family feeling with friendly companionship. Such a close relationship assumes that the members have several important things in common, though the individuals may be very different in other ways, and may not always agree with each other. What Christian fellowship offers above all is a relationship with God, often referred to as the Fellowship of the Holy Spirit. Within that over arching fellowship, human relationships based on Christian love are formed. It is true, of course, that some Christian groups appear more friendly than others to an outsider. However, closer acquaintance with a Christian group usually proves that there are welcoming hearts waiting to reach out to the stranger. To some extent a person joining a church has to be guided by their gut feeling that a particular one is right for them. This is a matter of temperament and feeling at home.

Like relationships within marriage, fellowship has to be fostered. Good fellowship will not happen unless people work at it. Helping each other at times of need, praying for each other, forgiving each other's weaknesses, meeting on other days than Sunday – possibly in people's homes, being tolerant of each other's idiosyncrasies, joining together on special occasions, working with each other to achieve an end and going out of one's way to speak to the shy person – all these aspects of fellowship are important. If the fellowship in your church is not what you think it ought to be, then do something about it!

When fellowship within a congregation is working properly, the atmosphere in that church radiates love and friendliness. It is hard when circumstances dictate that someone has to move out of that fellowship, perhaps because he has found a job elsewhere. However, that person knows that he will find fellowship in another Christian congregation near his new home. He also knows that it will take a while to build up new relationships.

8. Focus in life

What are we going to do today, or this week, or this year? Sometimes, of course, life gives very little choice. Work and the family seem to take up most of our time. However, even if there are limited choices at one stage in our lives, within that framework it is still possible to have a clear focus on what we do. For example, if we are trying to live by the law of Christian love, than our behaviour in all circumstances is going to focus on how to behave lovingly, though not over sentimentally. To change the focus slightly, we could consciously try to live according to God's will.

If at another stage in our lives we have less direct responsibility and more time to use and arrange as we wish, then the focus becomes critical. How are we going to use our time, our energy and our talents in the best possible way? Of course, we could enjoy frittering time away, and sometimes that is a good thing to do. Pottering about can be very therapeutic. However, in the ultimate there would be very little satisfaction or fulfilment in using all our time in that way. A person could make a conscious decision to direct his energies in a certain way. Possibly, for example, he might aim to be proactive in helping people and this might persuade him to work with others with like aims. Or to take another example, he might decide to use a gift he is dimly aware of, possibly in drawing and painting, and so he spends a good part of his time developing his skill and at the same time giving himself and other people pleasure. The same is true for other creative talents like music or poetry.

There is, in addition, the question of priorities. Somebody might define for himself several areas of interest or activity which he wishes to develop. Then he must think about these and decide how much time and energy he can give to each. If he is a praying person he will ask for guidance in his decisions. Furthermore, his belief in God will give him strong motivation to do his best in everything he attempts.

The main point is that, though people without religious beliefs can arrange their lives usefully and creatively, the Christian has a special power behind him. This power of God's active Holy Spirit in the world uses people to remove mountains.

9. Confidence

True confidence comes from deep within the mind and spirit. Christians with a strong faith know that God is with them and that nothing can ever separate them from God's love. St Paul put this very well when he wrote: *For I am sure that neither death, nor life... nor anything else in all creation will be able to separate us from the love of God in Christ Jesus our Lord.*[5] It is true that life may bring difficulties of all kinds; yet even at the worst times the love of God is always there. In fact, at the very worst times God may seem very close, as if he is suffering with us. With this inner certainty, each day can be faced with courage, whatever lies ahead. Even if it proves to a very busy day it is possible to "think" a short prayer when strength of spirit seems to be flagging. There are many words of Scripture which may be used as prayers. A very useful passage is to be found in the Book of

Isaiah: *They who wait for the Lord shall renew their strength; they shall mount up with wings as eagles, they shall run and not be weary, they shall walk and not faint.*[6]

10. Journey into mystery

Life is like a journey and in some respects mystery lies at the end of the journey for everyone. However, for the Christian the mystery lies at the end of what is only the first stage of a journey which continues into further mysteries. Eternal life is one dimension of the journey, but this is not limited to never ending time. In the Christian context, eternal life has many qualities as well as quantity. One of these qualities is the exploration of a relationship with the eternal being of God. Because God is both infinite and eternal, it is never possible to complete the journey. Ultimately God is impenetrable. However, he allows us to explore a relationship with him and in doing so reveals himself to us. To be conscious of the mysterious dimension in the here and now, is to have already begun the journey. In the next stage of life it can be postulated that this exploration deepens as God's mystery continues to unfold. This is one of the most exciting aspects of the Christian faith. We can behold many wonders now within God's creation: how many more wonders will we encounter in the new dimensions of the next life? St Paul could hardly wait to find out. He wrote, *My desire is to depart and be with Christ, for that is far better. But to remain in the flesh is more necessary on your account.*[7]

Concluding comment

This chapter has been about the advantages of being a Christian. These could be more accurately described as privileges. Along with these privileges go responsibilities.

To accept the privileges is to accept the responsibilities. What these responsibilities are will vary from person to person, depending on the gifts which each person has.

NOTES

1 Jesus proclaimed two laws to summarise the moral code: (a) Love God with all your heart; (b) Love your neighbour as yourself.
2 One copy of the Ten Commandments is to be found in the Book of Exodus, chapter twenty, in the Christian Bible.
3 See Matthew, chapter four, verses 1-11.
4 See Mark, chapter fourteen, verses 32-42.
5 See Romans, chapter eight, verses 38-39.
6 Isaiah chapter forty, verse 31.
7 Philippians, chapter one, verses 23b-24.

CHAPTER THREE

What is God like anyway?

1. How can God be a father?

Of course, she could just as well be a mother. However, the fact is that neither maleness nor femaleness identifies God. Parenthood, as we know, means that people procreate children, or bring them into being. But when does the child become a person? This could happen at any stage between conception and birth, and agreement on this question seems difficult to reach. Yet at some stage, that small bundle of flesh and bone does become a person. It may be that God brings this about by breathing his Spirit into the child. If this does happen, then that is clearly an aspect of God's parenthood. That, however, is difficult to prove.

Another aspect of divine parenthood is that God has created the human race and all the possibilities that lie in our genes. This does not necessarily contradict Darwinism. It is possible that God chose the way of evolution to create people, and this process may still be going on. Alongside that process of evolution each individual person may be evolving into a spiritual being, and that may define what life is all about. In that sense, God is our parent in the Spirit and eventually helps us to grow into the world of the Spirit, which is one way in which heaven may be defined.

God, then, can be our parent in at least three ways: firstly, when as babies we become persons; secondly, when God creates the whole of humanity through evolution; and thirdly, when we are fathered into heaven as spiritual beings. These three possibilities, of course, do not exhaust the depth of divine parenthood.

2. Who exactly is Jesus?

At the purely human level Jesus of Nazareth was a great teacher who, like Socrates, did not commit any of his wisdom to writing. It is only through the later records of his disciples that we know anything at all of Jesus' teaching. Tradition has it that he only taught publicly for about three years. Then he was crucified by the Roman authorities under pressure from the learned Jewish establishment. Little is known of Jesus' earlier life, though it seems probable that he helped Joseph, his reputed father, in his work as a carpenter. There is little reason to doubt these basic facts about the life of Jesus.

There are four portrayals of Jesus in four different Gospels (Good News stories). These have some similarities, but also have some significant differences. The stories in the Gospels show Jesus as a healer, as a miracle worker and as a popular teacher. However, all four Gospels claim that Jesus is God's eternal Son. The main event to authenticate this claim was the alleged appearance of Jesus after his death to some of his disciples. Two of the Gospels additionally claim that Jesus was born of a virgin called Mary, who married Joseph. The Gospels and other documents in the Christian Bible explain the death and resurrection of Jesus as God's way of showing his love and forgiveness to the world.

It is claimed by the Christian Church that Jesus Christ[1] exists eternally as God's Son and that he is, in fact, God, in one of God's three revealed personas. Thus, it is declared by the Church that God is One God who has Three Persons (or personas), namely Father, Son and Holy Spirit.

It could be argued that some aspects of the character and personality of Jesus are factual, while others are matters of faith. This duality parallels the Christian claim that God is both transcendent (beyond the world) and immanent (within the world). Jesus, then, was an Incarnation of God in the world, but has an eternal being in the Godhead. At the same time, it is claimed that Jesus was fully human when he lived upon earth. The relationship between the divine aspect of Jesus and the human one has caused many arguments, and most so-called heresies are departures from the present norm of Christian belief that Jesus was fully human, but was yet fully God's Son.

3. Who on earth is the Holy Spirit?

God, of course, is the Holy Spirit, and through this medium (or *persona*) he reveals himself to people today and works with them in the world. At the same time, the Holy Spirit is not usually obtrusive, but quietly influences events behind the scenes. Part of the divine mystery is that God does not go round in pomp and splendour. Rather, as the Incarnation of Christ shows, God acts as a servant. The majesty of God is hidden behind the humility of love. Once this is realised, it is very daunting for the believer. It means that he or she is also called to be a servant, both to God and to other people.

What sort of work, then, does the Holy Spirit do? He calls people into his service and he guides them in the work they feel called to do. Sometimes the Holy Spirit gives a command which so strikes the person at the receiving end that, he is full of awe and is compelled to obey. Like Jonah[2] he may try to disobey, but as happens in the poem *The Hound of Heaven*[3], he may feel in his conscience that God is pursuing him. Eventually he may find there is no escaping his responsibility to answer the call.

According to Christian belief as expressed in the creeds[4], the Holy Spirit is also the One who gives life and the One who guided the prophets of old to speak God's word. The first chapter of the Genesis story of creation describes the *Spirit of God*[5] upon the face of the waters before creation took place.

Many people testify to the work of the Holy Spirit in relation to themselves. When the Holy Spirit "speaks" (relates) to a person, the event is unmistakable and awe-inspiring.

4. How can God be three Persons?

Any of us can be three persons, but still be the one man or woman who shows himself or herself in three different ways. For example, a man may have a way of showing himself in the work place as a stern and uncompromising boss. The same man may show himself to his children as an old softie who loves them and plays with them. Yet again that man may also be a member of a golf club where he appears as a bit of a lad who enjoys a joke. In fact, it is better to use the word *persona*[6] to describe the different faces shown to different people by all of us.

In a similar way God has shown himself to us as three different Persons or personas. Of course, these revelations have been transmitted through individual people over several thousands of years. Because of the ways God has allowed such people to relate to Himself, He has been defined accordingly. The first three sections of this chapter have discussed briefly each of the three Persons God has shown, that is, Father, Son and Holy Spirit. These terms are from the Christian Bible, which was produced over a period of more than a thousand years. The New

Testament, which was composed from documents written and edited by different people over the first century AD and into the second century, is most revealing in the respect. Because it is believed the authors were inspired by God to produce these documents, the Bible is known as God's word. However, there are different interpretations among Christian groups as to what inspiration means in relation to the word of God.

The word Trinity is not used in the Bible, though the three Persons of the Trinity are mentioned together in several places. The Gospel of Matthew records the risen Jesus as saying, *Go therefore and make disciples of all nations, baptising them in the name of the Father and of the Son and of the Holy Spirit.*[7] As the Church reflected on the revelations recorded in the Bible, the word Trinity came into use to summarise the threefold nature of God's character.

Other aspects of the divine character are recorded in the Bible. For example, God is known as a Shepherd, as a King and as a Rock, to name but a few. In addition, it must never be forgotten that it is impossible for man to penetrate God's mystery completely. There are almost certainly many other aspects of God's character which are as yet unknown to man.

5. How does God show himself to people?

God may show himself to people in various ways, but as far as we know he has never appeared to anyone face to face, except in the form of Christ. Indeed, it does say in the Bible that, "no one has ever seen God."[8] Furthermore, when Moses asked if he could see God's glory, the answer was: "...you cannot see my face; for man shall not see me and live."[9] How then, does God show himself from the depth of his mystery?

Many people claim to have had some sort of sign

from God. Signs may come in various ways, for example, through dreams or visions, through miraculous phenomena, through hearing voices, through strange coincidences – to mention but a few of the possibilities open to an infinite and eternal God. Not surprisingly, there are some outstanding examples of special signs recorded in the Bible. The husband of the Blessed Virgin Mary, Joseph, had a vision of an angel who told him not to be afraid to marry Mary.[10] St Paul heard the voice of Jesus when he was struck to the ground on the way to Damascus.[11] Moses saw a burning bush in the desert, though the fire did not consume the bush. He also heard a voice.[12] St Peter was miraculously released from prison by an angel.[13]

But what of modern times? Do people still claim to have such experiences? One of the difficulties is that people are shy about discussing such very private matters openly, though their experiences may be shared with a few close friends. However, there have been some well known visions of the Virgin Mary, and these have usually been given to very ordinary and simple people. The places where such visions have occurred have often become places of pilgrimage. One example is the vision experienced by Bernadette Soubirous at Lourdes. Another is the vision given to three children at Fatima in Portugal. Both of these places are now famous, as are the stories of the people who had the visions.

Over Christian history there have been some very remarkable people. One of the most remarkable of these was St Francis of Assisi. Much of his story is familiar to non-Christians as well as to Christians. However, what is not quite so well known about him is that he bore the marks of Christ's crucifixion on the palms of his hands. These marks are called *stigmata*. This is a very special way in which God shows himself to a limited number of people.

Anyone who has not had a special experience of God may well be sceptical about the reality of such happenings. It may be true that sometimes people with vivid imaginations make false or exaggerated claims to have had a vision given by God or an angel. However, anyone who reads the story of Lourdes with an open mind, taking into account a number of authenticated healing miracles at the shrine, may have cause to ponder.

It is probably more common, however, for God to show himself to people in less spectacular ways. Sometimes a revelation of God's presence may be very subtle, like something seen out of the corner of the eye, or like a whisper of breeze on a calm day. Yet, such less obvious manifestations of God's presence are very convincing to the person on the receiving end, and they can be awesome.

Some of the biblical records about God's showing of himself are called theophanies. The word *theophany* means "God showing himself". Most people will be more familiar with the word *epiphany*, which has a similar meaning. In the story of Christ's birth the three *Magi*, representing the Gentiles, were privileged to have an epiphany when they saw the baby Jesus, and the season of Epiphany in the Church's calendar commemorates this event.[14]

6. How do I start to pray?

While there are many ways to pray, perhaps for the new starter there are three main choices:

  i. Use a set form of prayer
  ii. Pray in your own words
  iii. Have a few minutes of silence in an appropriate setting.

It is good to try different ways. Perhaps a combination of these three is a good starting place, that is, a silence, followed by a set prayer, and then some prayers in your own words. There are many books which provide set forms of prayer, but perhaps for a start the Lord's prayer with one other prayer might be sufficient. Try reading a verse from the Bible which you find particularly inspiring or helpful, for example, Isaiah, chapter forty, verse 31.

Where to pray and what posture to take are relevant questions. Choose a quiet place where you are unlikely to be interrupted. This may be anywhere in the house, or elsewhere. Whether to kneel, sit or stand when praying is an open question. Any of these postures may be appropriate, provided they are conducive to a relaxed form of prayer.

People who have prayed for many years find they are still exploring worship, so what is worship? Essentially it involves a relationship. The main ingredients are reverence and love. However, worship and prayer are like a beautiful landscape in an ever expanding stretch of countryside which reveals vista upon vista, surprise upon surprise, and revelation upon revelation.

7. How can God be confined by buildings or religious observances?

The answer is, of course, that God cannot be confined by anything or anyone, whether on earth or in heaven. But does that mean that God is not in the church building, and not in the sacrament of Holy Communion?

Church buildings are separated spaces where people can leave the world behind so that they can become more aware of God. People who go there have a separated space in their minds which their thoughts enter when their bodies enter the building. God reveals himself to the person who opens his mind in that way in that particular place. In that sense God is there, but only because he chooses to be there. Yet, some places seem to be holier than others. An ancient cathedral, for example, seems to have an aura of holiness because the person entering that space knows it has been used for worship for hundreds of years. The very stones are worn by people's feet. However, it is the mental space that is important, and when a religiously aware person enters that cathedral, a whole series of thoughts connected with holiness are switched on. While church buildings are human constructs they may well have been inspired by God in the first place. In any case, it is still legitimate to call a church "God's house", so long as it is remembered that God is over and beyond human thoughts or creations.

Does a similar argument apply to religious observances? Yes, but only in some respects. For example, to say a prayer is to enter a special space in the mind, and usually there is a corresponding area of space and time where this happens. For instance, if a person habitually kneels in a particular room to say his prayers at a particular time, then that environment encourages a prayerful attitude of mind. However, not all religious observances are of this kind. The sacrament of Holy Communion is not a human construct, except for the manufacture of the elements and the furniture of the church. What happens in Holy Communion is that the bread and the wine are in some mysterious way transformed into Christ's body and blood. Moreover, the sacrament was instituted by Christ himself at his last supper with his disciples. Yet, it is still true that God is not confined by the sacrament. God has chosen that way to have fellowship, or communion, with worshippers. It is an act of free grace on his part. At the same time, there are innumerable other ways in which God chooses to reveal himself to people.

8. How can God be both in heaven and on earth?

This is a particularly difficult question to answer when it is claimed that Jesus is the Son of God, a person in the Trinity, and an eternal part of God's being. How could a human being called Jesus live in Israel for between thirty and forty years and at the same time have been God?

In addition to that problem, there is the more general question as to how God is in some sense involved with the world he has created, when in fact he is over and beyond the world. There are two technical words used by theologians to describe this duality. It is claimed that God is both *immanent* (in the world) and *transcendent* (beyond the world).

One type of religious belief is to claim that God *is* everything. The theological word used to describe this view of God is *pantheism* (God is all). However, this is not the Christian view, which claims that God is different from the universe he has created, though he is active within it.

A solution to this problem conceived about two hundred years ago suggested that everything in the universe is somehow within God, though God's nature exceeds the universe. This was called *panentheism* (all in God).[15] To put this in simple terms, if God is compared with an infinite quantity of air, then the universe is like a small balloon of air filled by God. Or to use another comparison, if God is represented by a huge circle, then the universe is a tiny circle within the larger one. Yet again, it is reasonable to suppose that God is a thinking Being, though his thoughts are way beyond human thoughts. If it is accepted that God's thoughts brought the universe into being, then it exists in God's mind, but it takes up only a small segment of God's thinking. This last comparison helps our understanding in a number of ways. For example, it explains how God can be everywhere in the universe *(omniscient)*. It also explains how God knows what everyone thinks. In addition, it may explain how God can perceive our future.

Following on from this argument, each human being has a separate existence and freedom of choice. God releases each bubble of thought and spirit which is a newly born person and, though he is aware of what each person is doing, he does not usually interfere. However, when that person prays, God is immediately aware of the prayer and may or may not respond. It is as if each human being is attached to God by a kind of umbilical cord which also sustains something like electric currents which are the way people can communicate with God.

The ideas expressed above go a long way towards explaining how Jesus of Nazareth could be God Incarnate. His being as a human was still within the Godhead. He was given a separate existence and freedom of choice like everyone else. In other words he was fully human. However, the channel of communication between God and himself, though probably not different from yours and mine in structure, was surely more open. He could communicate with God the Father and God the Holy Spirit through his perfect prayers, contrasted with our imperfect prayers. Of course, such comparisons do not explain the wonder and mystery of the Incarnation, but they may help our understanding a little.

So in answer to the original question, God is both in heaven (beyond the world) and on earth all the time and he does not have to move up or down or in any direction to be in either place. However, if heaven is some further dimension which people can explore after this life, then that too is within God, though the relationship between God and the saints and angels may well be much deeper than ours. In a sense, when we die we are still in God's thoughts and our transfer from one sphere to the other may be, as St Paul suggests, "in the twinkling of an eye."[16]

9. How could anyone create out of nothing, a universe as complex and as beautiful as the one in which we live?

Well, of course, it is a great mystery as to how someone could create a computer and invent something as complex as the Internet! These are just two examples of human creations, which are many and varied. Anyone who has created even something small knows that there is a sheer joy in creating a new thing. A good starting point for answering the original question then may be: how do people come to have such capacity for creation?

It is true, of course that people do not create things out of nothing, though creative ideas sometimes seem to appear from nowhere. This process is usually referred to as inspiration. But an actual new creation, whatever it may be, is created from given materials or forms. Music is created from a system of sounds, and the musical instrument may be made from a variety of materials, most of which have themselves been created from so-called raw materials. Even the world of ideas, from which new ideas may be created, uses forms based originally on the senses. The creative human organism itself is a given. The body and the brain combine to create many wonders.

However, all the creative possibilities that we possess as human beings have themselves been created by God. This means that the Creator must have creative thoughts. He thinks, therefore he is. But if the universe did not at one time (?) exist, how could it be brought into existence? There is the theory of the big-bang, of course, and God may have caused the big bang. But God must have a way of thinking things into existence so that where nothing was, something now is.

We understand what creativity is, so to that extent we can understand what is meant when we say God created the universe. But how can you make rocks and stones by thinking them? Or how can you make atomic structures by dreaming them up? That, perhaps, is the point. God's creative power has a capacity which human creativity does not have – at least not yet. God can bring things into existence out of himself. As said in a previous section, all things, including the universe, are in God anyway, or at any rate in his mind. If all the structures of the universe as we know it, including ourselves, are in God's mind, then the process of creation is a little more comprehensible. I can imagine all kinds of things, for example, mathematical problems; but they may remain in my mind and never be communicated to anyone. This could be similar to the way in which God's creative thinking works.

The Bible does actually state something like that. Chapter one of Genesis claims that God said (thought) "Let there be…" and the universe was brought into being.

10. How does God show his love?

If we are loved by someone in our own family, the signs of that love are usually plain to see, despite the fact that some people do have difficulty in showing their feelings. Human love is shown by physical contact or by actions which the loved person should appreciate, though sadly it is sometimes the case that love is not appreciated. This may be very hurtful for the person showing such love. Is the love of God different from human love and can we recognise it? We may or may not appreciate the love that God has for us, but how do we know it exists?

Love, of course, is an emotion and the essence of love may be experienced at a spiritual level. Some may say, "That's all very well for the great mystics like Julian of

Norwich, but my prayer life is very ordinary and I'm not good enough to know God's direct love like that." The answer to that is a simple one, for love is simple. Any person of any age may have this experience by opening his or her heart to God. A short silence, while praying with the heart and mind open to the love of God, is one way of approaching this. The love of God is tangible in the soul and it embraces the deepest parts of consciousness. Sometimes, indeed, there may be an overwhelming physical experience, for emotion has its physical manifestations.

God's love may also be shown in practical ways, that is, through events. Perhaps this is a matter of interpretation to some extent. However, many people testify to a perception of God's actions in their lives. Sometimes this is understood at the time, though at other times the love of God in a particular event may only be known with the wisdom of hindsight. This is true of the way God answers prayers. Sometimes an answer is specific and very obvious. At other times God's response to the prayer is perceived much later. Quite often God's love is shown to us through the loving actions of people around us.

The greatest act of God's love that we are aware of, happened in the life, death and resurrection of Jesus. It is obvious from the Gospel stories that Jesus performed many acts of love and compassion to those around him. However, how God's love was shown on the cross is a very complex question and this is dealt with in a later chapter. Suffice to say for the moment that the highest ideal of love is sacrificial. At the human level, for example, parents make sacrifices for their children because they love them. God's love is also sacrificial.

According to the First Letter of John, "God is love".[17] This means that whenever a human being shows love he or she is in some sense expressing the essence of God in the world. Christian love is more than sentimental or romantic love, though these have their place in God's wonderful creation. A perceptive description of love is given by St Paul in his famous hymn to love.[18] The passage ends with these words: "So faith, hope and love abide, these three; but the greatest of these is love.

NOTES

1. The word *Christ* means *Messiah* or *anointed one*.
2. The short book of Jonah in the Jewish Scriptures part of the Christian Bible tells the story of a man who knows he is called to be a missionary to Nineveh. However, he tries to escape by boarding a ship. Through a strange series of events, including being swallowed by a whale, he eventually fulfils his mission.
3. The poem is by Francis Thompson.
4. There are three main Christian creeds, or statements of belief. The shortest of these is called *The Apostles' Creed*.
5. The Book of Genesis, chapter one, verse 2. The Hebrew words translated as *Spirit of God* are sometimes translated *wind of God*, because the word for *spirit* in Hebrew is the same as the word for *wind*.
6. Defined by the Oxford Compact English Dictionary (1996) as "an aspect of the personality as shown to or perceived by others".
7. Matthew, chapter twenty-eight, verse 19.
8. John, chapter one, verse 18.
9. Exodus, chapter thirty-three, verse 20.
10. Matthew, chapter one, verses 20-21.
11. Acts, chapter nine, verses 4-6.
12. Exodus, chapter three, verses 1-6.
13. Acts, chapter twelve, verses 1-11.
14. In the Eastern Church, Epiphany is associated with the baptism of Christ.
15. The word *panentheism* was first used by K.C.F. Krause (1781-1832).
16. See First Corinthians, chapter fifteen, verses 51-52.
17. Ibid., chapter four, verse 8.
18. Ibid., chapter thirteen.

II
God's self-portrait

The title of Part II has been chosen to show that God has revealed himself to people in particular ways. Thus, the Bible, if it is God's word, gives a self-portrait of God, transmitted through a range of gifted people who received divine revelations. However, it has to be remembered that people are fallible and capable of error, which means that our view of God can never be perfect.

Each chapter draws out from the biblical text some aspect of God's nature. This is followed in each case by a discussion of the practical implications for people in their every day lives.

CHAPTER FOUR

Father figure

What the Bible has to say

The idea of God as Father has already been mentioned briefly in a previous chapter. This theme is developed more fully in the present chapter.

The false picture of God as an old man with a beard probably grew out of a misunderstanding of God's Fatherhood, which incidentally is a very ancient idea. God was seen as a Father by Jewish people long before Jesus was born. Descriptions of God as Father may be found in the Jewish Bible, which is a collection of pre-Christian writings. The Christian Church refers to this collection as the Old Testament, which is not a very complimentary way to describe the sacred book of another faith. In fact, the Scriptures read by the early Christians were the Jewish Scriptures. The New Testament was another collection of writings put together by the Church many years after Jesus had died. In this book the first part of the Christian Bible will be referred to as the Jewish Scriptures while the second part will be referred to as the New Testament.

So what do the Jewish Scriptures say of the Fatherhood of God? The prophet Malachi writes: *Have we not all one father? Has not one God created us?*[1] This perceptive statement shows that the Fatherhood of God is about his creating the human race as a whole, and each one of us as a separate being. If God made the universe and everything in it, this must be true. God must have had a reason for creating people and one of the usual answers is that he did it out of love. This means he loves us and that we have the opportunity to love him.

This aspect of God's nature is clearly expressed in the Jewish Scriptures. For example, the author of one of the Psalms puts forward the idea that God is a *compassionate Father*.[2] Many people are fortunate enough to have a human father who is loving and compassionate, though unfortunately some children have less understanding parents. However, if we imagine human fatherhood at its very best, then that gives us an inkling as to what God the Father might be like. Of the many things that fathers do, one is to watch over their children and to give advice or support, but at the same time to give them a growing responsibility and freedom to organise their own lives. God does this all of this in a wonderfully loving way. The people portrayed in the Jewish Scriptures were fully aware of this. The idea that the God of the Jewish Scriptures is only a wrathful and unfeeling judge is false.

However, the psalmist does write: *As a father pities his children, so the Lord pities those who fear him.*[3] The Hebrew word for "fear" used here also means to honour or reverence. In fact, it is true that fear of God's judgement arises from a realistic appraisal of what life is about. We are accountable at the end of our lives for everything we have done. But God's judgement goes along with his mercy and compassion.

Apart from God's Fatherhood, there is a similar comparison between God's care and love to a mother's feeling for her children. The prophet Isaiah writes: *Can a woman forget her suckling child, that she should have no compassion on the son of her womb? Even these may forget, yet I (God) will not forget you.*[4] The point is that very few mothers would ever stop thinking and caring about their babies – but God's love is even greater than a mother's. This comparison with a mother emphasises that God may be compared to a parent of either sex, though ultimately his Fatherhood does not fall into human categories, though to see him in this way helps us to understand him.

The Psalms contain other insights about God's Fatherhood. Psalm 89 mentions King David, and the psalmist writes: *He (David) shall cry to me, 'Thou art my Father, my God, and the Rock of my salvation.'*[5] One important point about David, though, is that the Bible portrays him as capable of doing great wrong, as when he stole another man's wife and arranged for the man to be killed in battle.[6] Furthermore, God's word to him is that if any of his sons are sinful, then God will punish them; yet at the same time God will not stop loving them.[7] This is very much what any conscientious father would do. Children who have strayed need to be helped, but may also need to be dealt with sternly. The Book of Proverbs, which contains much practical advice, makes this very point. The author writes: *My son, do not despise the Lord's discipline or be weary of his reproof, for the Lord reproves him whom he loves, as a father the son in whom he delights.*[8] The compassionate element in God's Fatherhood is very much illustrated by another psalmist who writes: *Father of the fatherless and protector of widows is God in his holy habitation.*[9] Interwoven throughout many stories and poems of the Jewish Scriptures is this knowledge of God's concern for deprived people.

Another aspect of divine Fatherhood in the Jewish Scriptures is expressed by the belief that it was God who brought the nation of Israel into being.[10] Along with that idea goes the thought that the Jewish people were especially chosen by God, not because they were powerful or mighty, but because he loved them and also because he had made a promise to Abraham, the father of the Jewish people.[11] This means that God chose a weak and small nation as the medium for his revelation to the world, which is parallel to the way that Jesus, as God's Son, showed God's love through humility and suffering.

The New Testament has a great deal to say about the Fatherhood of God. He is described by Jesus in the *Lord's Prayer* as being in heaven.[12] Now what this means is subject to interpretation. In biblical times heaven was thought to be above the sky because they believed in three levels of existence – heaven above the earth, and hell below. Our view of the world is different. We can only assume that heaven and hell are spiritual dimensions beyond the earth. Possibly they are also states of mind. In any case, to say that God is in heaven means he is mysteriously beyond our world as well as being in it. Statements about where God has his existence can only be symbolic.

St Paul's thoughts about the Fatherhood of God are interesting, especially when he writes: *For this reason I bow my knees before the Father, from whom every family in heaven and on earth is named, that according to the riches of his glory he may grant you to be strengthened with might through his Spirit in the inner man, and that Christ may dwell in your hearts through faith...*[13] This is one of the places in the New Testament where Father, Son and Holy Spirit are mentioned together, almost as a team. However, the idea of the Trinity is discussed in a later section, so that aspect of Paul's thought will not be discussed here.

What is fascinating is that he asserts that every family in heaven and on earth is named from the Father. This may mean a number of things. It could mean, for example, that human fatherhood is based on the pattern of God's Fatherhood, and that this is also true of families in heaven.

Leaving aside the heavenly element, which is beyond our immediate understanding, this means that just as God has brought all the families that exist into being, so earthly fathers play their part by bringing their children into being.[14] A further dimension of this idea may be that Jesus Christ the Son is eternal. This could mean that God has made us in the image of Jesus Christ, that is, as his sons and daughters.

The relationship of Jesus with God the Father during the period of the Incarnation is a fascinating one. Some of the Jewish establishment hated Jesus for his assumption of authority. Not only did he knowingly break the Sabbath rules, but he also *called God his own Father.*[15] Their hatred of Jesus made them want to kill him and, of course, they eventually did. Jesus seems to have had this special relationship with God the Father since he was a child. When Joseph and Mary took Jesus to Jerusalem for the Passover they found on the way home that Jesus was not with them. When they went back to search for Jesus they found him having a serious discussion with some learned teachers. Mary expressed her anxiety, but Jesus said calmly: *Did you not know that I must be in my Father's house?*[16]

The closeness of Jesus' relationship with God is well illustrated by the form of address he sometimes used when speaking to God. In the garden of Gethsemane Jesus prayed that he would not have to drink the bitter cup of death on the cross. He prayed: *Abba, Father, all things are possible to thee; remove this cup from me; yet not what I will, but what thou wilt.*[17] *Abba* means something approximating to the English *Daddy*. After his prayer Jesus realised that it was necessary to go through with the Passion to complete his work on earth.

God our Father in the here and now

It is a wonderful experience to be loved by someone. At the human level, there is usually a lot love in a family. For example, there is the love of a man for his wife, or children for their parents or parents for their children. If family relationships are tied in with God relationships, then the family members are living in a community of God's love. For the single person the love of a divine Father is even more wonderful. There is no need ever to be lonely, because when the heart is opened to the Father's love there is a warmth of feeling which is unmistakable. However, perhaps a key is needed to open the self to God. This may be in a prayer-talk with the Father or it may happen during a quiet activity at home, or when listening to some music, or while looking at an icon, or in some other way. Customarily prayers are addressed to the Father, as in the prayer that Jesus taught his disciples, though this does not exclude The Son or the Holy Spirit, for the three members of the Trinity are themselves an indivisible community of love. With many people, simply to kneel and say *Father* may be a way to open the self to the love which is always there, the love which never fails. Words are not essential to know the Father's love.

It is not easy to analyse love and, indeed, to experience it is much more important than attempting to dissect it. However, it is manifest that care and compassion, forgiveness and renewal, constancy and accessibility represent some important aspects of love. One of the stories told by Jesus provides a deep insight into what a father's love means. This is the parable about the son who left home and wasted his life and his inheritance. Yet, when he returned home his father's love was still burning steadily and the son was forgiven and reinstated in the family.[18] This, of course, gives a very clear picture of what God's fatherly love is like. We may stray far away from him, but he will always welcome us with love when we return.

The story also illustrates that a good father allows his sons to make their own decisions and to learn by their mistakes. God does not dictate what we have to do, though he does give moral guidelines in the Commandments listed by Moses[19] and the two all embracing laws recommended by Jesus.[20] Life has a way of teaching hard lessons, but however much of a mess we may have made, God will always welcome us lovingly. This applies to small matters and to great ones. If we have had a bad day we can turn to the Father for comfort. If we have had a serious disaster in our lives, we can ask the Father's help. It is at our worst times that the Father is most loving towards us.

A human father sometimes has to indicate that his children have done wrong, or sometimes he has to bail them out. The relationship with God is similar. To pray to the Father with a seriously guilty conscience, but without trying to make amends, is to risk a temporary break up in the relationship. However, to be in trouble and to ask for help at the very least, will bring God's perspective into the situation. This may lead to strength of mind to deal with the problem; or peace of mind to live with the difficulty; or it may lead to direct help from an unexpected quarter. For example, if someone is told he is in the early stages of cancer, he may have to undergo uncomfortable and sustained treatment. To pray to the Father about this may result in learning to live with the possibly serious consequences of the illness; or it may lead to a deep inner peace with the knowledge that whatever happens God is within the situation; or it may be that the dedicated work of medical staff brings about a remission of the cancer. God's help is never failing, though the help may come in unforeseen ways.

To pray to the Father about the route our lives seem to be taking, may lead to a deeper understanding of what God's plan is for us. Sometimes, in retrospect, the development of God's plan for the individual can be perceived. Once the direction is clear, then further prayers will help the journey along that road. However, it is possible to take the wrong road and not to realise it until much later. This is less likely to happen if prayer is a constant in our lives. It may be that God has a blueprint for each person who is born, and to grow according to the plan of that blueprint may be the main purpose of our lives upon earth. To put this in another way, seeking to do God's will is surely one of the key features of our relationship with the Father. A woman might believe she has a vocation to be a nurse, but marriage and children prevent her from going in that direction. After a few years, when the children are older, she realises she wants to be a doctor. Eventually this proves to be God's will for her.

Praying to the Father opens the gate of heaven in the here and now. We can actually live in God's kingdom each day as we go along, and we can feel that we are borne on the wings of angels. Heaven is in the mind and heart and, however unattractive our surroundings may be, the reality of God being with us is compelling. Yet, just as a tap may be turned on or off, we can turn off the God connection ourselves if we are not persistent in our prayers. God himself will never turn off the tap. Whether we are praying privately, or taking part in community worship, God is potentially with us. If, with Jesus, we can say *Abba Father*, and try to hold the closeness of that relationship, God's love will always be with us and nothing except our own stupidity can ever take it away from us.

One of the Commandments forbids us to make images of God. At the time when the Ten Commandments were written, the worship of manufactured images was always a temptation to believers. Such temptations may still be with some people, depending on the circumstances of their lives. However, how do we picture God mentally, especially when we pray? It is probably easier to have a picture of Jesus in mind, than it is to visualise God the Father, though in art there have been portrayals of a father figure. This is a very personal matter and different people may find different ways of achieving this. Some may not try to picture God at all, but leave him as a blank space, so to speak. On the other hand, poetry and art may provide a rich symbolism which helps a person to pray. Provided such images are regarded as stimuli and not as portraits of God, then they may be helpful.

NOTES

1 Malachi, chapter two, verse 10.
2 Psalm 103, verse 13.
3 Ibid.
4 Isaiah, chapter forty-nine, verse 15.
5 Psalm 89, verse 26.
6 The full story of David and Bathsheba may be read in 2 Samuel chapters eleven and twelve.
7 2 Samuel, chapter seven, verses 14-15.
8 Proverbs, chapter three, verses 11-12.
9 Psalm 68, verse 5.
10 See Jeremiah, chapter three, verse 19 and chapter thirty-one, verse 9.
11 See Deuteronomy, chapter seven, verses 6-8.
12 See Matthew, chapter six, verse 9. See also Matthew, chapter twenty-three, verse 9.
13 See Ephesians, chapter three, verses 14-17.
14 In the Greek text of the letter the word *pater* is used for *father* and the word *patria* is the word translated as *family*. This could be a deliberate pun on Paul's part – if he wrote his letter in Greek.
15 John, chapter five, verse 18.
16 Luke, chapter two, verses 41-51.
17 Mark, chapter fourteen, verse 36. Originally *Abba*, an Aramaic word, was an address by very young children to their fathers. By New Testament

times it was used even by older children and sometimes in addressing elderly men. See *Exegetical Dictionary of the New Testament, Vol. I*, eds. H. Balz and G. Schneider, T & T Clark, 1990, pp. 1-2.
18 Luke, chapter fifteen, verses 11-32.
19 See Exodus, chapter twenty.
20 See Luke, chapter ten, verses 25-28.

CHAPTER FIVE

Everybody's brother

This chapter explores what it means to say that Jesus Christ is the Son of God. Along with that, the complementary idea that all of us are children of God is also discussed. Firstly an investigation into what the Bible says about the subject will be made, and then the practical implications will follow in the second part of the chapter. This is such a complex topic that only a selection of the main themes can be explored.

What the Bible has to say

The Jewish Scriptures foreshadow the Sonship of Christ in several ways. For example the Davidic king was believed to be God's son in some sense. In Psalm 2 the poet writes: *I (the king) will tell of the decree of the Lord: He said to me, 'You are my son, today I have begotten you.'*[1] It is generally accepted by commentators that this sonship was believed by the Israelites to be an adoption by God of the ruling king, and that this gave the king a special place as God's vicegerent upon earth. However, the New Testament writers take this to be a prophecy about Christ as Son of God. Paul quotes this text in one of his sermons as such a prophecy.[2] The author of Hebrews also quotes the text for a similar reason, but in the same verse quotes from the Book of

Samuel: *I will be his father, and he shall be my son.*[3] This was originally about David's royal descendants, but it also is interpreted in the New Testament as a Christological statement.

In a more general way, the nation of Israel is described in the Jewish Scriptures as God's first born son. That is how Moses described Israel to Pharaoh.[4] Israel was Jacob's other name and so, the grandson of Abraham gave his name to the Hebrew people. This fulfilled the promise to Abraham that he would be the father of many people. The prophet Hosea uses a similar description of his people: *When Israel was a child, I (God) loved him, and out of Egypt I called my son.*[5] This text is quoted in Matthew's Gospel to show that the journey of Mary and Joseph to Egypt was a fulfilment of the prophecy of Hosea.

In Isaiah there is mention of a son who will be named *Prince of Peace*. This is a famous passage often used in Christmas carol services. The text reads: *For to us a child is born, to us a son is given; and the government will be upon his shoulder, and his name will be called 'Wonderful Counsellor, Mighty God, Everlasting Father, Prince of Peace.'*[6] Of course the passage does not read *Son of God*, but it is generally taken by Christians to refer beforehand to Christ as God's Son. In a similar category comes the Immanuel prophecy in Isaiah: *Therefore the Lord himself will give you a sign. Behold, a young woman shall conceive and bear a son, and shall call his name Immanuel* (God-with-us).[7] Isaiah was probably referring to a coming son of the reigning king, Ahaz, the son being Hezekiah. However, Matthew's Gospel uses the text to point to Jesus as God's son.[8]

Jesus often referred to himself as the *Son of man*. On the face of it these words would apply to any man as a *son of Adam*. Indeed Ezekiel referred to himself frequently as *son of man*.[9] Some of the Psalms use this form of words. The most famous example is in Psalm Eight where we read: ...*what is man that thou art mindful of him, and the son of man that thou dost care for him?*[10] Although the *son of man* is described in the following verse as little less than God, and as one who is crowned with glory and honour, the reference is clearly to humanity as a whole. In rather a different category comes the mention of a *son of man* in the Book of Daniel. The prophet writes: ...*and behold with the clouds of heaven there came one like a son of man, and he came to the Ancient of Days*[11] *and was presented before him. And to him was given dominion, and glory and kingdom, that all people, nations and languages should serve him*...[12] Jesus himself speaks of the *Son of man:* ...*then will appear the sign of the Son of man in heaven...and they will see the Son of man coming on the clouds of heaven with power and great glory.*[13] The title *Son of man* is ambiguous, because it can refer to any man, but it also came to mean God's Son in a special way. Sometimes Jesus used the title ambiguously, but with his disciples he was more open. For example, when Peter declares that Jesus is Christ, Jesus explains that the *Son of man must suffer many things.*[14] His use of this title of himself was regarded as blasphemous at his trial before the high priest: *And the high priest asked him, 'Are you the Christ, the Son of the Blessed?' And Jesus said, 'I am; and you will see the Son of man seated at the right hand of Power...'*[15]

There are frequent references to Jesus as the Son of God throughout the New Testament. For example, in his introduction to his letter to Rome, Paul writes that he is set apart '*for the gospel of God which he promised beforehand through his prophets in the holy scriptures, the gospel concerning his Son, who was descended from David according to the flesh and designated Son of God...*'.[16] At his baptism Jesus was presented as God's *beloved Son.*[17] Similarly, when three disciples witnessed the Transfiguration of Jesus they heard a voice saying, *This is my beloved Son, with whom I am well pleased; listen to him.*[18] The author of John's Gospel explains that he wrote his book *that you may believe that Jesus is the Christ, the Son of God...*[19] Paul is explicit when he writes of Jesus *...who though he was in the form of God, did not count equality with God a thing to be grasped, but emptied himself, taking the form of a servant...*[20] Many more examples could be given to show that the New Testament writers regarded Jesus as God's Son. However, it is inappropriate in a short book to delve into too much detail.

Even so, a few comments about the function of Jesus as the Son of God would be appropriate. The easiest way to do this in a short space is to tabulate some of the functions attributed to Jesus, giving at least one biblical reference in each case. In most cases there are many more references that could be used and these can be found in any biblical concordance.[21] Some of the implications of ideas mentioned in the table will be "unpacked" in the second part of the chapter or in later chapters.

Biblical picture of Christ

Jesus Christ, the name above all names	Luke 1:30-33
	Philippians 2:9-11
God Incarnate (literally *in the flesh*)	John 1:14;
	1 Timothy 3:16
A pattern of manhood to follow	Luke 9:23
God's Word	John 1:14
A wonderful teacher	Matthew 5-7
	Luke 10:25-37
	Luke 15:11-32
A healer	Mark 5:21-43
	Luke 5:12-16

A miracle worker	John 2:1-11
	Mark 5:35-43
	John 11
Redeemer	Luke 1:68
	Luke 21:28
	Galatians 3:13
The One who atones for sin	Romans 5:11-18
Saviour	Luke 1:47
	Luke 2:11
	John 4:42
	Matthew 1:21
	John 3:17
	Ephesians 5:23
	2 Peter 1:11
A ransom for many	Mark 10:45
	1 Timothy 2:6
One who justifies us	Romans 3:24
Reconciler	Romans 5:10
	Colossians 1:20
Prophet	Luke 21:5-36
	Mark 13
	Matthew 23-24
Servant	John 13:12-20
	Mark 10:35-45
Announcer of God's kingdom	Mark 1:15
	Mark 9:1
The One who rose from the dead	Mark 16
	Matthew 28
	Luke 24
	John 20-21
Jesus is High Priest in heaven	Hebrews 4:14
A living sacrament	1 Corinthians 11:23-26
	Mark 14:22-25

The Bible makes it clear that we may all of us become sons or daughters of God. In the Beatitudes, which are part of Jesus' great Sermon on the Mount, it is written: *Blessed are the peacemakers, for they shall be called sons of God.*[22] This text shows that sonship is conditional on how we behave. Paul also suggests that we have to behave in a certain way in order to be children of God. He writes: *Therefore be imitators of God, as beloved children.*[23] He goes on to explain that *walking in love* is the way to achieve this. In his letter to the Romans Paul takes this idea further when he claims that as children of God we are fellow heirs of God with Christ, provided we suffer with him in order to achieve glory. In Luke's Gospel Jesus speaks of the resurrection and shows that our destiny after death is to become equal to the angels and to become sons of God.[24] This implies that our status as God's children becomes perfected in the resurrection. The moral aspect of being a son of God is clarified by the author of the Book of Revelation. He writes: *He who conquers shall have this heritage, and I will be his God and he shall be my son. But as for the cowardly, the faithless... and all liars, their lot shall be in the lake that burns with fire and sulphur, which is the second death.*[25] This language is symbolic, and not to be taken literally, but it is clear that immoral behaviour will be punished in some way. To be a child of God, then, is a wonderful opportunity for all of us, but for those who choose to walk away from God, hard lessons lie in store.

Jesus is one with us

God wished to show people what he is like, so what did he do? He decided to portray himself in human form so that we could clearly see his love in action. This is an amazing thing to do, for the Creator of the universe to live a human life in a humble home among ordinary people. Not only does the incarnation help us to understand some aspects of God's character but at the same time we can associate ourselves with him in a realistic sense. Jesus worked for a living until he began his ministry; he had friends and enemies; he suffered pain; he helped people; he had temptations; he knew hunger and thirst; he had brothers and sisters; and he awoke to each new day after a refreshing sleep. In the main, these are experiences we all have. However, his was a short life which ended in tragedy, but out of that tragedy emerged the most influential movement in human history, the growing and changing Christian Church.

We know little of the early life of Jesus, but we have a vivid picture of his short ministry in the four Gospels. Some of his teaching has been preserved and, because of the way disciples in those days learned by rote, there is a strong probability that at least the Sermon on the Mount and the parables reflect his teaching accurately. There is a wealth of practical advice in this teaching and certainly over the centuries the thoughts and actions of many people have been profoundly affected by what Jesus said. In fact, as far as we know he did not himself leave any written records.

The recorded actions of Jesus have also been very influential. He called people to follow him, then, as he still does today. He healed many people from various infirmities, including leprosy and demon possession (mental disturbance). He brought people back to life, for example, Lazarus, who had been dead for several days.[26] He lived a life of poverty, depending on providence to grant his needs. He performed miracles which showed his power over nature, and still performs miracles to this day, often in answer to prayer. He berated people for hypocrisy and greed, but forgave an adulterous woman. He cut to the heart of true morality by casting aside outdated traditions. He made friends with people who were despised by others. He served people with humility, as when he washed the feet of his disciples as an example. He suffered torture, humiliation and death to serve mankind, even though he was innocent of any crime. While dying painfully on the cross, he forgave his enemies. This pattern of living and dying has inspired many people over two thousand years to try to imitate Jesus in their own way of life, and there have been some outstanding examples of saints who have lived Christ-like lives. St Francis of Assisi and Mother Teresa are two examples of such dedication. While it is true that not many of us could aspire to those standards, nevertheless our lives can be changed by Jesus, and in our behaviour we can at least make a small beginning in trying to conform with Christly standards.

Christ enables us to approach God by acting as a Mediator between God and humanity. Even though he was, is, and always has been God, his humanity was no pretence. In all respects he was a human being. That is one of the reasons why many prayers are offered *through Jesus Christ our Lord.* Christ understands our needs and draws us into an active relationship with God. Through Christ we can be reconciled with God whatever wrongs we may have done. Through Christ we can be forgiven for our sins. Through Christ our lives can be changed, redeemed and saved for heaven. (The raft of ideas related to redemption is considered in detail in chapter ten of this book.)

Jesus is the focus for Christian worship. He is characterised as the high priest in heaven, but he is also in the sacrament of Holy Communion, which is the most important act of worship in mainstream churches. Those who take part are remembering Christ at his last supper and on the cross, where he shed his blood and where his body was shattered in a painful death. However, the act of communion is more than remembering, for the bread and the wine are in a mysterious way the body and blood of Christ. There are different interpretations as to how Christ is present in the sacrament, but for many people the theological differences are less important than the reality of Christ through the elements. It is an amazing privilege to communicate with God in this way and, as said above, this takes place through the mediation of Christ. Furthermore, the communion is not only with God, it is also with each other, and those who take part are in a true sense part of a family, brothers and sisters in Christ. (Worship is further discussed in chapter fourteen of this book.)

Perhaps the most important aspect of the practical work of Christ is that he has made known to the world that there is a resurrection after death. His appearances to his disciples, recollected between Easter and Ascension Day, were a pronouncement that through Christ we are drawn into a new life when this one is complete. In fact, the new life starts here and now for those who accept that Jesus is Lord. This is a process of growth and the door of death opens to allow further development of the soul in a different dimension. It is as if a seed were planted into our earthly bodies and then transplanted into heavenly bodies. The relationship between the earthly and the heavenly in this context is mysterious. However, when the body of Christ was renewed in the tomb there may have been a merging of the earthly and the heavenly. This would account for the seeming inconsistencies in Christ's resurrection appearances, for he came to his disciples sometimes as a spirit, sometimes in the flesh. In any case, the glory of the heavenly world is a new country for advancing souls to explore.

NOTES

1 Psalm 2, verse 7.
2 Acts, chapter thirteen, verse 33.
3 2 Samuel, chapter seven, verse 14; Hebrews, chapter one, verse 5.
4 Exodus, chapter four, verses 22-23.
5 Hosea, chapter eleven, verse 1.
6 Isaiah, chapter nine, verse 6.

7 Ibid., chapter seven, verse 14.
8 Matthew, chapter one, verse 23.
9 See for example Ezekiel, chapter twenty-three, verse 36 – and throughout the book.
10 Psalm 8, verse 4.
11 Generally taken to be God.
12 Daniel, chapter seven, verses 13-14.
13 Matthew, chapter twenty-four, verse 30.
14 Mark, chapter eight, verse 31.
15 Ibid., chapter fourteen, verses 61-62.
16 Romans, chapter one, verses 1-3.
17 Matthew, chapter three, verse 17.
18 Ibid., chapter seventeen, verse 5.
19 John, chapter twenty, verse 31.
20 Philippians, chapter two, verses 6-7.
21 For those not familiar with this type of book, a concordance is a dictionary of biblical terms which gives biblical references.
22 Matthew, chapter five, verse 9.
23 Ephesians, chapter five, verses 1-2.
24 Luke, chapter twenty, verses 34-36.
25 Revelation, chapter twenty-one, verses 7-8.
26 See John, chapter eleven, verses 5-44. See also Luke, chapter seven, verses 11-17.

CHAPTER SIX

The ghost in the machine

What the Bible has to say about the Holy Spirit

The idea of the Spirit of God is central throughout both the Jewish Scriptures and the New Testament, but only a small number of incidences are discussed here. There is one significant difference between the Jewish Scriptures and the New Testament. The Holy Spirit (traditionally the Holy Ghost) is used extensively as a title for God in the New Testament. However, the Jewish Scriptures do not use this title, though there are many references to God's Spirit and at least one interesting reference to the Spirit of holiness.[1]

God's Spirit appears right at the beginning of the Bible story in the creation account in the Book of Genesis which reads: *...and the Spirit of God was moving over the face of the waters.*[2] The words for *spirit* in both Hebrew and Greek mean *wind* as well as *spirit*, so other translations of this text include *the wind of God* or *a mighty wind*. Be that as it may, the writer of the passage was surely fully aware of this ambiguity. The comparison between the wind and the spirit is a very rich one and is discussed further below.

In the Jewish Scriptures the Spirit is described as relating to people in various ways. These include, for example: the Spirit of God coming upon someone; being taught by the Spirit; being filled with the Spirit; being transported by the Spirit; receiving God's word by the power of the Spirit.[3] One important example quoted in the New Testament comes from the prophecies of Joel.[4] He writes: *And it shall come to pass afterward, that I will pour out my Spirit on all flesh; your sons and daughters shall prophesy, your old men shall dream dreams, and your young men shall see visions. Even upon the menservants and maidservants in those days, I will pour out my Spirit.* This passage is used by St Peter on the day of Pentecost to explain the behaviour of those who had been filled with the Holy Spirit. Passers-by think they have drunk too much wine, but Peter denies this and cites the Joel passage as a prophecy fulfilled on that day.

The Day of Pentecost is a Jewish festival and because a special manifestation of God's Spirit happened on that feast day Christians use the same name for a festival in their calendar. The history book called Acts of the Apostles, probably written by St Luke, is sometimes called the Gospel of the Holy Spirit, partly because it is this book which gives an account of what occurred on the Day of Pentecost, and partly because the Holy Spirit is a major character in the events recorded in the book. One very important event described by Luke is the so-called gentile Pentecost. This was the occasion when the Holy Spirit came upon non-Jews in a spectacular way.[5] As on the Day of Pentecost the people endowed with the Holy Spirit began to speak in tongues. In the earlier account of Pentecost this way of speaking is described in detail: *And they were all filled with the Holy Spirit, and began to speak in other tongues, as the Spirit gave them utterance.*[6] Luke explains that the people around, who were from many different countries, identified their own languages among those spoken. Some Christian churches practise speaking in tongues today, though St Paul advocates caution in this respect.[7]

Jesus, of course, prophesied the coming of the Holy Spirit. According to John's Gospel, Jesus said: *These things I have spoken to you, while I am still with you. But the Counsellor, the Holy Spirit, whom the Father will send in my name, he will teach you all things, and bring to your remembrance all that I have said to you.*[8] Earlier in the chapter from John, the Counsellor is called *the Spirit of truth.*[9] The word translated as *Counsellor* is the Greek word *parakletos (paraclete).*[10] Sometimes this is translated as *Comforter* or *Advocate.* Literally the word means *one called upon for help.* This refers to the Holy Spirit's role as guide and help. Later in the Gospel Jesus is reported as saying: *When the Spirit of truth comes he will guide you into all the truth…and he will declare to you the things that are to come.* This means that to certain chosen people the Holy Spirit will reveal future events. There are several examples of this happening in Acts of the Apostles. Peter, for example, after he had had a strange vision, was told that three men were looking for him and that he should go with them.[11] The future events foretold by the Spirit could include the Second Coming of Christ or the End Time (Last Things).

There are several symbols which represent the Holy Spirit. Two of these are described on the Day of Pentecost as wind and fire: *And suddenly a sound came from heaven like the rush of a mighty wind, and it filled all the house where they were sitting. And there appeared to them tongues as of fire, distributed and resting on each one of them.*[12] As mentioned earlier, the Greek word for "spirit" (*pneuma*) also means "wind". Fire is associated in the Jewish Scriptures with divine revelations, as when Moses had a vision of a burning bush.[13] Another symbol for the Holy Spirit is the dove. This arises from the description of the baptism of Jesus in the first three Gospels. Matthew, for example writes, *And when Jesus was baptised, he went up immediately from the water, and behold, the heavens opened and he saw the Spirit of God descending like a dove, and alighting on him...*[14]

According to Matthew and Luke, the Blessed Virgin Mary had a unique experience of the Holy Spirit when she became pregnant without having had sexual intercourse with her fiancé, Joseph. Matthew writes: *When his mother Mary had been betrothed to Joseph, before they came together she was found to be with child of the Holy Spirit...*[15] Luke's account describes an annunciation by the angel Gabriel, who says to Mary: *The Holy Spirit will come upon you, and the power of the Most High will overshadow you; therefore the child to be born will be called holy, the Son of God.*[16] Belief in the Virgin Birth is one of the most important teachings of the main Christian denominations.

St Paul describes the special gifts of Catholic people as gifts of the Holy Spirit. He gives at least two lists of these, which are each different from the other, so the list is not a closed one and applies to the work of Christians in general under the guidance of the Holy Spirit. In his first letter to the Corinthian Church Paul writes: *Now there are varieties of gifts, but the same Spirit...to one is given through the Spirit the utterance of wisdom, and to another the utterance of knowledge according to the same Spirit, to another faith by the same Spirit, to another gifts of healing by the one Spirit, to another the working of miracles, to another prophecy, to another the ability to distinguish between spirits, to another various kinds of tongues, to another the interpretation of tongues. All these are inspired by one and the same Spirit, who apportions to each one individually as he wills.*[17] This idea of spiritual gifts serves to emphasise that the Holy Spirit is working through the Church and its people.

The Holy Spirit is our guide and help

Just as the Incarnation of God's Son was an act of God in the world, so the Day of Pentecost was another act of God to show God's active interest in human affairs. The two events support each other to reveal to all the human race that God is not a distant figure, but that he is close to us and working with us towards our respective destinies. The work of the Holy Spirit is not confined to the Church, although many would claim that the Day of Pentecost was the day on which the Church was founded. This last may be true, but God's Holy Spirit cannot be confined by any human institution. Even within the Church, the Holy Spirit does not attach himself to any one denomination. Any group of people who trust in God and pray for guidance will be heard by God and his Holy Spirit will somehow show the way forward. One of the pitfalls in the Church is to believe that God is confined to a building, to an organisation, to a book or to an act of worship. God is certainly present in all of these, but he is also present and active in many other spheres.

How does a person know that the Holy Spirit is within the realm of his or her experience? How do we know that such claimed experiences are not just creations of the human imagination? Well of course the imagination may be involved, as may the intellect or the emotions or the body. The Holy Spirit speaks in many different ways, but when a person is aware of the action of the Holy Spirit he is not likely to forget the experience. However, such experiences are not directly transferable, and other people may well be sceptical.

Of course, the Holy Spirit is God and if someone has a deep sense of the holiness of God, then the Holy Spirit of God is within him. The natural human reaction is reverence and awe. Some people report that they have had other kinds of experience probably involving the

Holy Spirit. It is not always clear in such experiences whether the Holy Spirit is directly at work, or whether some angelic presence is involved. However, angels are God's messengers, so they do represent the Holy Spirit. As in biblical times, people in more recent times have had dreams or visions. One well-known example is that of Bernadette Soubirous who had a vision of the Virgin Mary at Lourdes. In a similar way, St Joan of Arc heard angelic voices guiding her.

Other people may have mystical experiences similar to that of Elijah in Mount Horeb[18] or to that of St Paul when he was transported to the third level of heaven.[19] More common perhaps, is a sense of exhilaration and a strong feeling that the Holy Spirit is all around and within. This happens sometimes in public worship in some churches. Sometimes combined with such spiritual elation is the experience of speaking with tongues. This seems like an overflowing of the Spirit as happened at the first Pentecost. Indeed, some churches call themselves Pentecostal churches because they are aware of direct experiences of the Holy Spirit.

Another manifestation of the Holy Spirit's work is in his guiding signs. Sometimes these may be spectacular as when Constantine the Great, the night before a battle had a dream or vision of a cross, and took this as a sign of God's favour, so much so that he had a cross put on his standards. (Another version claims that Constantine had a vision of a cross in the sky.) He went on to defeat his enemies and became the first Christian Roman emperor. More likely, for most people, signs for guidance are unobtrusive to the casual observer, but may be very clear to the person concerned.

For example, when Augustine of Hippo was sitting in his garden one day with a book on his knees, he heard a child's voice calling *Open and read, open and read.* When Augustine opened the book the first words he read were from St Paul's letter to Rome: *But put on the Lord Jesus Christ, and make no provision for the flesh, to gratify its desires.*[20] This experience changed his life and he later became a famous bishop and theologian.

Many people today testify to experiences similar to that of St Augustine, though there is a tendency to be reticent about such matters, except among close Christian friends. Here is an adaptation of the real experience of a man who was seeking guidance as to whether or not to follow a particular Christian vocation. After he had prayed earnestly for guidance, he opened his Bible and the first words he read were: *You did not choose me, but I chose you and appointed you that you should go and bear fruit and that your fruit should abide...*[21] Two days later he went to a Sunday service in a church where he was not well known. One of the lessons read during the service included the words he had read in his Bible. He found this very convincing and believed that God's word had come to him through the Holy Spirit and, encouraged by other signs, he decided to study to be a priest. Unfortunately, opening the Bible in that way does not always bring about a convincing countersign, and so it is as well to be cautious about interpreting any particular text. There is a well-known text in the Bible which indicates that the Spirit moves freely according to his will, which means that people cannot predict or tie down the Holy Spirit. It was Jesus himself who said, *The wind (= spirit) blows where it wills, and you hear the sound of it, but you do not know whence it comes or whither it goes; so it is with every one who is born of the Spirit.*[22]

The gifts of the Spirit are many and varied, but within church congregations some gifts are more obvious than others. For example, preaching, pastoral care and teaching are obviously gifts from God. On the other hand, some less obvious gifts are also from God, for example, the people who arrange flowers or clean the church are doing important work for God in that particular place. However, the gifts of the Spirit are not confined to members of the Church. Inspiration comes in many ways, and the creation of beautiful forms in art or literature is surely divinely inspired. Many other gifts, of course, are given to people outside church circles. Serving the needs of people in a loving way, for example, is not the prerogative of Christians. At the same time, people using "natural" gifts may not perceive them as coming from God, but if God did create the universe and all things within it, then the varied gifts that people possess are surely God given.

NOTES

1 See for example Psalm 51, verse 11 (Hebrew verse 13). The phrase used in this psalm is sometimes translated as *holy spirit*. Some commentators argue that the phrase refers to the divine principle in man.
2 Genesis, chapter one, verse 2.
3 For examples of each of these, see Isaiah, chapter sixty-one, verse 1; Nehemiah, chapter nine, verse 20; Exodus, chapter thirty-one, verse 3; Ezekiel, chapter thirty-seven, verse 1; Zechariah, chapter four, verse 6.
4 Joel, chapter two, verses 28-29.
5 Acts, chapter ten, verses 44-48.
6 Ibid., chapter two, verse 4.
7 1 Corinthians, chapter fourteen, verse 9.
8 John, chapter fourteen, verses 25-26.
9 Ibid., verses 16-17.
10 For a full discussion of the word see *Exegetical Dictionary of the New Testament Vol. III*, eds. H. Balz and G. Schneider, Eerdmans, 1993, pp. 28-29.
11 Acts, chapter ten, verses 19-21.
12 Ibid., chapter two, verses 2-3.
13 Exodus, chapter three, verse 2.
14 Matthew, chapter three, verse 16.
15 Ibid., chapter one, verse 18.
16 Luke, chapter one, verse 35.

17 1 Corinthians, chapter twelve, verses 4-11 and see Ephesians, chapter four, verses 1-14.
18 1 Kings, chapter nineteen, verses 9-12.
19 2 Corinthians, chapter twelve, verses 1-4.
20 Romans, chapter thirteen, verse 14.
21 John, chapter fifteen, verse 16.
22 Ibid., chapter three, verse 8.

CHAPTER SEVEN

Threefold mystery

It is a strange but undeniable fact that the word Trinity is not used to describe God anywhere in the Bible. The history of how the doctrine of the Trinity became central to Christian belief is interesting, but complex, and only a few threads of the story can be taken up here.[1]

What the Bible has to say

Scholars have identified possible references to the Trinity in the Jewish Scriptures, though these are somewhat tenuous. In the Book of Genesis, for example, God is presented as speaking of himself in the plural when the author writes: *Then God said, 'Let us make man in our own image, after our likeness...'*[2] This is an oddity which has never been satisfactorily explained, though some have suggested that it is an example of the *royal we*. Strangely the most common word for God used in the Jewish Scriptures is a plural form (Elohîm). This has sometimes been described as a plural of majesty. Another example sometimes quoted in this context is the story of the three angelic visitors to Abraham's tent who announced that the barren Sarah would have a child.[3] Yet again, there is *the Thrice-holy* poem in the book of Isaiah. This poem has been adapted for Christian hymns. It reads: *Holy, holy, holy is the Lord of hosts; the whole earth is full of his glory.*[4] A further example lies in the Prince of Peace prophecy in the book of Isaiah, which reads: *...and his name will be called Wonderful Counsellor, Mighty God, Everlasting Father, Prince of Peace.*[5] While this prophecy is on the surface about a coming king in the Davidic dynasty, it has often been taken as a prophecy about the coming of Christ. Deeper consideration shows that the Wonderful Counsellor could refer to the Holy Spirit, the Everlasting Father to God the Father, the Prince of Peace to Christ, and Almighty God to the whole Trinity in One. The Holy Spirit works in mysterious ways and this may be a revelation by God about his Trinitarian nature through Isaiah's prophetic word.

In the New Testament the so-called Trinitarian formula appears. This is especially important in Matthew's Gospel where the risen Jesus is described as instructing his disciples. He says, *Go therefore and make disciples of all nations, baptising them in the name of the Father and of the Son and of the Holy Spirit...*[6] This indicates that the three Persons of the Trinity were associated as One in very early times in the history of the Church. Another important example is placed at the end of Paul's second letter to Corinth. Paul ends his letter with these words: *The grace of the Lord Jesus Christ and the love of God and the fellowship of the Holy Spirit be with you all.*[7] After the Lord's Prayer, this is one the most popular prayers in the Christian Church. Paul also writes in another letter: *And because you are sons, God has sent the Spirit of his Son into our hearts, crying, 'Abba! Father!'*[8] In the first Letter of Peter we read: *Peter, an apostle of Jesus Christ...chosen and destined by God the Father and sanctified by the Spirit for obedience to Jesus Christ...*[9]

John's Gospel clearly associates the three Persons of the Trinity in a number of places, though not necessarily as a sacramental formula. According to John, Jesus says to his disciples as part of his long farewell discourse: *These things I have spoken to you, while I am still with you. But the Counsellor, the Holy Spirit, whom the Father will send in my name, he will teach you all things...*[10]

It can be seen, then, from the above examples, that the Church was justified in concluding from the New Testament writings that the Son and the Holy Spirit are One with the Father.

The concept of Trinity in the early Church

This section contains only a brief summary of a tiny proportion of the issues involved in the development of the doctrine of the Trinity. As far as possible technical terms have been avoided.

The main problem has always been based around the tension between the Threeness and the Oneness of God. How can One God be three Persons, or how can Three persons be expressed in one God-head. The first recorded use of the Greek word for Trinity (*trias – triados*) was by Theophilus of Antioch who was active in the late second century AD.[11] The Trinity he described consisted of God, his Word and his Wisdom. Wisdom is taken to refer to the Holy Spirit, though at times Wisdom is also ascribed to the Word. This idea, of course, is not quit the same as the usual concept of Trinity. However, Theophilus represents only a stage in the growth of Trinitarian definition, though his thoughts are nevertheless interesting.

The Christian Creeds are normally in three parts, one concerning the Father, one concerning the Son and one concerning the Holy Spirit. The earliest creed may be the Apostles' Creed (see page 174), though it was most probably not written by the twelve apostles of Jesus. It is first mentioned by St Ambrose c. 390 AD, though it is believed to depend on a previous creed called the Old Roman Creed which can be traced back as far as the end of the second century. The threefold form is believed to be based on the baptismal command of Jesus recorded by Matthew mentioned above.[12]

In 325 AD the Emperor Constantine called the Council of Nicea. This Council defined the Nicene Creed which is commonly used today in Eucharistic worship. It also is in three sections, each devoted to a Person of the Trinity. The Nicene Creed was formulated to defend what became orthodoxy against a group called the Arians who denied the full divinity of Christ. Most of the so-called heresies of early Christian times tended to over emphasise either the divinity or the manhood of Christ, thus losing the balance. A sceptic might argue that orthodoxy was the view of the side that won the argument and that it could have gone the other way. However, many Christians would accept that the Councils were guided in their formulations by the Holy Spirit.

Attempts to define the Trinity have been many and varied. Some saints or scholars have produced very simple explanations. St Patrick, for example, is reputed to have compared the Trinity to a cloverleaf, a single leaf with three parts. A group called the Cappadocian Fathers[13] produced a more complex theory in the late fourth century. They were present at the famed Council of Constantinople in 381 AD and also argued against the Arians. Their idea was that God is One being with three Hypostases.[14] Gregory of Nyssa, a member of the group, wrote that *God is divided without separation and united without confusion.*[15]

St Augustine of Hippo concluded that the Trinity is like the mind. He wrote: *We held, therefore, that a trinity of the mind is to be intimated also by these three terms, memory, intelligence and will.*[16] In a long and complex argument he uses various faculties of the mind to illustrate that in the one human being there can be three aspects of mind at work, just as in the One Godhead there can be three Persons working as One.

People today are still producing analogies to try to explain the nature of the Trinity. For example, a man can show a different persona to different groups of people. To his family he may show himself as a loving father. To his own parents he may appear as a son who cares about them but keeps himself at a distance. To his colleagues he may appear as a cold and efficient administrator. In a similar way, goes the argument, God can show himself in at least three Personas, as the Father, as the Son and as the Holy Spirit.

The old so-called heresies still arise, but the churches hold to the traditional creeds. Nevertheless, some church people have difficulty in believing everything that the creeds assert. However, those who do accept the creeds as they stand often argue about how the various clauses should be interpreted. In a way, the creeds have defined the problem of the Trinity, though they have not solved it. This is not surprising, because the mystery of God is ultimately impenetrable.

What does the Trinity mean to us?

The obvious value of the Trinity idea to Christians is that they can perceive God in at least three different ways and this helps them to understand what God is like. As already explained, God's creative power is shown through his Fatherhood; his love and redemptive power are shown through the Son; the wisdom of God and his willingness to guide us are shown through the Holy Spirit. This, of course, does not exhaust the functions of the three Persons of the Trinity, as shown above. However, it is useful to have headline summaries.

A great advantage of the Christian Three-in-One God

is that prayers may be said to any of the three Persons without excluding the other two. If somebody prays their thanks to the Father for all the good gifts he has in his life, then the Son and the Holy Spirit are also addressed. Similarly, if somebody prays to Christ to be forgiven for his sins, then the Father and the Holy Spirit are part of the love that is in that situation. Then again, if a prayer is addressed to the Holy Spirit to ask for guidance about an application for a job, then the Father and the Son are part of the guiding process. Many prayers, of course, include all three persons of the Trinity. It is customary to mention the Father at the beginning of a prayer, and then at the end to mention Jesus Christ and the Holy Spirit. For example a prayer might read like this:

Father, I ask for your help and strength to go through the day that lies ahead with determination and direction. Abide with me in all I think or speak or do, and bring me to the end of the day with a clear conscience and a peaceful heart. I ask this in the name of your Son, Jesus Christ, and through your most Holy Spirit. Amen.

Jesus does say that we should pray in his name: *If you ask anything in my name, I will do it.*[17] He also says that he is the Way, the Truth, and the Life, and that *no one can come to the Father except through me.*[18] However, he also says: *And I will pray the Father, and he will give you another Counsellor, to be with you forever, the Spirit of truth...*[19] This close community within the God head is encouraging. We are drawn into that community of love, and through the Son and the Holy Spirit we learn godly love in the world, and we learn to turn to the Father of all creation each day as we live our lives surrounded by God's love.

NOTES

1. Books and articles on the Trinity abound. For those who wish to read a short but detailed account, see: *The International Standard Bible Encyclopedia Vol. Four,* General Editor G.W. Bromiley, Eerdmans, 1988, pp. 914-921.
2. Genesis, chapter one, verse 26.
3. Ibid., chapter eighteen, verses 1-15.
4. Isaiah, chapter six, verse 3. This poem is entitled the *Trisagion*, which means *Thrice-holy*.
5. Ibid., chapter nine, verse 6.
6. Matthew, chapter twenty-eight, verse 19.
7. 2 Corinthians, chapter thirteen, verse 14.
8. Galatians, chapter four, verse 6.
9. 1 Peter, chapter one, verses 1-2.
10. John, chapter fourteen, verses 25-26. See also chapter fifteen, verse 26.
11. See "Ad Autyculum" 2:15, in *The Anti-Nicene Fathers Vol. II,* eds. A. Roberts and J. Donaldson, T & T Clark, 1994 reprint.
12. Matthew, chapter twenty-eight, verses 19.
13. Including St Basil the Great, St Gregory of Nazianzus and St Gregory of Nyssa.
14. The word *hypostasis* came to mean an *individual reality*.
15. See "Contra Eunomium", ii 2 in *Nicene and Post-Nicene Fathers, Second Series, Vol. V,* ed. P. Scaff and H. Wace, T & T Clark, 1994 reprint, p. 102.
16. See "De Trinitate", xiv 6, in *Nicene and Post-Nicene Fathers, First Series,* Ed. P. Schaff, T & T Clark, 1993 reprint, p. 187.
17. John, chapter fourteen, verse 14.
18. Ibid., verse 6.
19. Ibid., verse 16.

III

History is more than a book

The chapters in this section explore some of the most important Christian themes from a historical perspective. The idea of God's word and the wonders of prophecy are discussed in relation to the Incarnation of God's Son. The potential effects of Christ's work are described with biblical examples, together with a discussion of how these impinge upon the practicalities of the Christian life. A long view of history is outlined from the time of the call of Abraham to the present day; and then the aim of history and its future implications for all of us are explored. These discussions enable the Christian to place his own life in the context of the divine revelation.

CHAPTER EIGHT

Just a few words

The Bible is known among Christians as the word of God, but what does this mean? Is it that in the Bible we are able to read about God through his revelation, as explained in Part Two of this book? Certainly this is part of the picture, but God's word is a much more complex idea than that. This chapter will explain the various implications of belief in *God's Word*.

The biblical view

First of all, the written words of the Bible do not represent the original form of God's Word. Before the documents of the Bible were written in Hebrew, Aramaic and Greek, a whole range of people were involved in recording and editing; but even before that stage, special people had the awesome experience of being spoken to by God. They felt that their experiences had to be shared, so poets wrote psalms, prophets spoke or wrote their oracles and these were preserved, historians interpreted the meaning of events with God's action as their main perspective, teachers collected wise sayings, parables and allegories were written to express spiritual ideas, evangelists told the story of Jesus, church leaders wrote letters to congregations to inspire or admonish them. These are some of the aspects of God's word to be found in the Bible.

Some of the biblical writings indicate clearly that they were believed to be inspired by a special word from God. Most of the prophets in the Jewish Scriptures used traditional forms of words like, *Hear the word of the Lord* or *The word of the Lord came to me...* For example, the prophet Amos begins one of his oracles with these words: *Hear this word that the Lord has spoken against you, O people of Israel...*[1] He also precedes an oracle with the words, *Thus says the Lord...* [2] In both cases he castigates the people for their bad behaviour. The prophets also speak God's word in hopeful oracles. Jeremiah, for example, writes, *Behold the days are coming, says the Lord, when I will make a new covenant with the house of Israel...*[3]

Not surprisingly, human nature being what it is, some prophets claim falsely to be speaking God's word. For example, a prophet called Zedekiah, and all the professional prophets with him, prophesy that the kings of Israel and Judah will win a forthcoming battle. Zedekiah says, wearing horns on his head as a symbol of victory, *Thus says the Lord, 'With these (horns) you shall push the Syrians until they are destroyed.* However, the true prophet of the day, Micaiah, tells the kings they will be defeated.[4] According to the author of the book of Deuteronomy, a true prophet may be distinguished from a false prophet by whether or not his word comes true.[5]

Another interesting point about God's word to prophets is that the word can be *seen*. In other words, a vision can be God's word of revelation. Isaiah, for example, introduces an important oracle with these words: *The word which Isaiah the son of Amoz saw concerning Judah and Jerusalem.*[6] Similarly, Amos introduces his book of prophecies in this way: *The words of Amos, who was among the shepherds of Tekoa, which he saw concerning Israel...*[7] Of course, more frequently the word of God was *heard* by a prophet. This may be symbolic, but there are places where a prophet claims to have heard the voice of God or that of an angel. Elijah, for example, when on Mount Horeb, had a strange experience, but part of that experience was actually hearing God's voice. The historian writes in the first Book of Kings: *And behold there came a voice to him (Elijah), and said, 'What are you doing here, Elijah?'*[8]

Perhaps the prophet Malachi is one of the best illustrations in the Bible of the belief that God communicates with prophets. The very first words in his book are *The oracle of the word of the Lord to Israel by Malachi.*[9] The name Malachi actually means *my messenger.* It is impossible to say whether this was the prophet's actual name, although people at that time did adopt symbolic names. However, this description is used later in the book, possibly to describe the prophet Elijah who was expected to come before the Messiah: *Behold, I send my messenger to prepare the way before me...the messenger of the covenant in whom you delight, behold he is coming...*[10] This is made more interesting by the second last verse of the book which reads: *Behold I will send you Elijah the prophet before the great and terrible day of the Lord comes.*[11] Christians take this to be a reference to John the Baptist who, it is claimed, prepared for the coming of the Messiah.[12]

The idea of speaking God's word is taken up in the New Testament, often in relation to preaching the Gospel, a word which means good news.[13] In the history of the early church as recounted in the Acts of the Apostles, it is decided to appoint seven men to be *deacons* or servants of the people. The writer explains: *It is not right that we should give up preaching the word of God to serve tables. Therefore, brethren, pick out seven men of good repute, full of the Holy Spirit, whom we may appoint to this duty.*[14] To this very day, preaching is seen as presenting God's word, and usually involves interpreting God's word in the Bible. Paul sees his teaching as a presentation of God's word: *Let him who is taught the word share all good things with him who teaches.*[15] Whether or not today's preachers and teachers may be regarded as prophets is a different matter. To some extent this depends on how the word is defined, but then there is no simple definition of what a biblical prophet is. Was John Henry Cardinal Newman a prophet, or was Martin Luther a prophet? There are people who would make claims for either or both of these men to be classed as prophets.

Mark precedes his Gospel with the deceptively simple statement: *The beginning of the gospel of Jesus Christ, the Son of God.*[16] The whole of the book, then, is seen as God's good news, or God's word, embodied in Jesus. Paul also sees the word of Christ as internal to each person: *Let the word of Christ dwell in you richly, teach and admonish one another in all wisdom...*[17] This is reminiscent of Jesus' explanation of the parable of the sower. He told his disciples: *The seed is the word of God...and as for that in the good soil, they are those who, hearing the word, hold it fast in an honest and good heart, and bring forth fruit with patience.*[18] The letter of James emphasises this idea. The author writes: *Be doers of the word, and not hearers only, deceiving yourselves.*[19]

There are many other interesting comments on God's word throughout the Bible, but there is only room to mention a few of these. One of the psalmists writes: *Bless the Lord, O you his angels, you mighty ones who do his word, hearkening to the voice of his word.*[20] This indicates that angelic beings exist and that one of their functions is to act upon God's word. Quite often, according to Christian belief, this involves bringing messages to people in this world. It is significant that after the Virgin Mary had been told by Gabriel that she was to have a child who would be a great king, she said, *Behold I am the handmaid of the Lord; let it be to me according to your word.*[21]

God's word is also seen as fixed and eternal. In the book of Isaiah it is written: *The grass withers, the flower fades; but the word of our God will stand forever.*[22] This is presented in the context of the prophet answering God's call to announce a special revelation of the divine glory. The first letter of Peter in the New Testament quotes this text and adds: *That word is the good news which was preached to you.*[23] Further to this idea, Jesus himself announces that his own words are eternal. In prophesying the coming of the Son of man, he says, *Heaven and earth will pass away, but my words will not pass away.*[24]

The most amazing expression of God's word is Jesus himself in the Incarnation. John introduces his Gospel with these words: *In the beginning was the Word, and the Word was with God, and the Word was God.*[25] This reminds the reader of the creation story in the first chapter of Genesis when God created the universe by his word. Later in his prologue (foreword) John writes, *And the Word became flesh and dwelt among us, full of grace and truth...*[26] The Greek word used for *word* is *logos*, and many English words are derived from this. Some theologians argue that John's use of the word *Logos* is borrowed from Stoic philosophy in which the *Logos* is claimed to be the divine principle existing in the world and giving it unity. To be sure, John seems to be using the *Logos* to describe Jesus in a similar way.

What God's word means today

God's word in the Jewish Scriptures is, of course, a guide and help to many Jews and to many Christians. In addition, the Christian New Testament contains a vital declaration of God's word to all Christians. Sometimes a particular text seems appropriate to the circumstances. In the Jewish Scriptures, for example, these words from a psalm have comforted countless people, including many who have no direct religious affiliation: *Even though I walk through the valley of the shadow of death, I fear no evil; for thou art with me; they rod and thy staff, they comfort me.*[27] Furthermore, a verse or text may hit somebody hard because it strikes at either the conscience or the sense of vocation. The author of the letter to the Hebrews writes: *For the word of God is living and active, sharper than any two edged sword, piercing to the division of soul and spirit, of joints and marrow, and discerning the thoughts and intentions of the heart.*[28] Many people in the modern world find this to be true. Suppose, for example, a man is heavily criticising another man for his behaviour. From out of the blue the critic comes across this text: *Judge not, that you be not judged.*[29] This has an immediate impact and the critic realises that he has been unfair in his judgement.

Many of the stories in the Bible provide guidelines for human behaviour today. Some are fictional, such as the story of the Good Samaritan who helps a man in dire need.[30] Some record actual events, such as the story of how David has an adulterous affair and arranges for the woman's husband to be killed in battle. The prophet Nathan tells him a parable which brings home to the king how evil his behaviour has been.[31] Some stories may be based on life, but they may also have been embroidered by an author. The story of Joseph and his brothers in the Jewish Scriptures may come into this category. One lesson that may be learned from this story is the strength of family love when forgiveness comes after a dispute. Joseph eventually forgives his brothers even though they had sold him into slavery.[32] In the New Testament, the historian, Luke, who probably wrote Acts of the Apostles, may have had to use his imagination in some parts of his history. For example, it is unlikely that he knew verbatim what St Stephen said in a long speech just before he died, so Luke has seemingly written something appropriate after talking to Paul or other witnesses to Stephen's martyrdom. The story of Stephen is an inspiration to Christians in any age who are threatened with persecution.

However, God's word today is not confined to the Bible. God speaks to us afresh just as he spoke to the prophets and apostles. There are several ways in which this may happen. For example, the voice of conscience can be very powerful and Christians believe that this is a God given faculty. Another way in which God's word comes to people is when they pray, possibly for comfort or for guidance. Events have a way of bringing the answer to such prayers and people are often convinced that God's word has come to them in this way. Take, for example, a woman who prays for a baby but then finds it is impossible for her to have a child. A friend suggests to her that she may become a foster parent, and over the years she helps several children by giving them a good home. She may realise afterwards that God has indirectly answered her prayer in his own way, by bringing his word to the situation.

It may seem sometimes that God does not speak to people in special ways as he did in biblical times. However, people in modern times have claimed to have had visions or to have heard God's voice. Although many people have no experience of such direct communications, perhaps it is well to keep an open mind on the subject.

NOTES

1. Amos, chapter three, verse 1.
2. Ibid., chapter three, verse 12.
3. Jeremiah, chapter thirty-one, verse 31.
4. 1 Kings, chapter twenty-two, verse 11-17.
5. Deuteronomy, chapter eighteen, verses 21-2.
6. Isaiah, chapter two, verse 1.
7. Amos, chapter one, verse 1.
8. 1 Kings, chapter nineteen, verse 13.
9. Malachi, chapter one, verse 1.
10. Ibid., chapter three, verse 1.
11. Ibid., chapter four, verse 5.
12. See Mark, chapter one, verses 2-3.
13. A translation of the Greek word *euangelion* from which the word evangelical is derived.
14. Acts, chapter six, verses 2-3.
15. Galatians, chapter six, verse6.
16. Mark, chapter one, verse 1.
17. Colossians, chapter three, verse 16.
18. Luke, chapter eight, verses 9-15.
19. James, chapter one, verse 22.
20. Psalm 103, verse 20.
21. Luke, chapter one, verse 38.
22. Isaiah, chapter forty, verse 8.
23. See 1 Peter, chapter one, verses 23-25.
24. Matthew, chapter twenty-four, verse 35.
25. John, chapter one, verse 1.
26. Ibid., verse14.
27. Psalm 23, verse 4.
28. Hebrews, chapter four, verse 12.
29. Matthew, chapter seven, verse 1.
30. Luke, chapter ten, verses 25-37.
31. 2 Samuel, chapters eleven and twelve.
32. Genesis, chapter forty-five, verses 1-15.

CHAPTER NINE

With foresight

Did the most important event in world history happen without notice? In other words, did God warn people of the Incarnation, or not? There is a lot of evidence to suggest that warnings were given, but that most of these were only understood with hindsight. It is, of course, to the Jewish Scriptures that Christians have to look to find such evidence. Jewish people, however, would interpret the warning signs in a different way. For example, it is part of Jewish belief that the Messiah is still to come.

People generally think of prophets when they consider the question of foresight. The prophets of the Jewish Scriptures were teachers, but they also foretold events within their own history up to the time when their Scriptures were complete. Several examples of such foresight are recorded in the Book of Isaiah. The prophet foretold that King Ahaz's wife would have a son who would be a great king.[1] This came true in the person of Hezekiah, one of the few kings praised by the biblical historian. Yet again, when Jerusalem was under siege by the Assyrians, Isaiah told King Hezekiah that the city would not fall. He said, *Therefore, thus says the Lord concerning the king of Assyria: he shall not come into this city, or shoot an arrow there, or come before it with a shield, or cast up a siege mound against it.* Surely enough, the Assyrians had to retreat because of a deadly sickness among the soldiers.[2] Later in the book of Isaiah, another prophet, usually known as Second Isaiah, prophesied that his people would return from exile in Babylon at the will of the conquering Persian king, Cyrus.[3] This came about shortly afterwards. Of course, it could be argued that these stories were recorded after the events they describe and that they were doctored by editors. However, it seems unlikely that godly people would concoct falsehoods, especially in view of the strong Mosaic ethic which guided all the Jews, and still does.

The question is, can the argument be carried further to show that there were prophecies of the coming of the Messiah which came true in Jesus of Nazareth? One prophecy already mentioned in the previous paragraph was interpreted in that way by the early Christians. Matthew, in his Gospel, writes of the birth of Jesus: *All this took place to fulfil what the Lord had spoken by the prophet: 'Behold, a virgin*[4] *shall conceive and bear a son, and his name shall be called Emmanuel'*.[5] A further question is, what was in the prophet Isaiah's mind when he spoke these words? Undoubtedly he was thinking of a young woman of his own time, but was he inspired by God to speak words with a deeper meaning than he realised? If this was the only example of such a prophecy, then this might seem unlikely, but when all the messianic prophecies are considered, the work of the Holy Spirit acting beforehand may be seen quite clearly.

There are several other significant kingship prophecies in the book of Isaiah. The prophet describes an ideal king, descended from Jesse through King David, upon whom the Spirit of the Lord will rest. The coming king will have *the spirit of wisdom and understanding, the spirit of counsel and might, the spirit of knowledge and the fear of the Lord.*[6] A similar description is the Prince of Peace prophecy already mentioned in connection with Christ as the Son of God (page 70). This passage also puts an ideal gloss on the expected king: *Of the increase of his government and peace there will be no end, upon the throne of David, and over his kingdom, to establish it and to uphold it with justice and righteous from this time forth and forevermore. The zeal of the Lord of hosts will do this.*[7] Unfortunately, no Israelite king proved to be ideal, though some were no doubt better than others. This meant that the hope for the ideal king tended to be focused on the future, hence the claimed application of the prophecies to the coming of the Messiah.

The Lord's anointed (the Messiah) is also described in a late addition to the book of Isaiah. The author writes: *The Spirit of the Lord is upon me, because the Lord has anointed me to bring good tidings to the afflicted; he has sent me to bind up the broken hearted, to proclaim liberty to the captives, and the opening of the prison to those who are bound; to proclaim the year of the Lord's favour...* Jesus famously read this passage from the Scriptures in the synagogue at Nazareth, and his comment is, *Today this scripture has been fulfilled in your hearing.*[8] It seems obvious that Jesus applied the kingship prophecies of the Jewish Scriptures to himself.

The ideal king is also described in some of the psalms, known as royal psalms. Some of these may have been written for the inauguration of new kings, and it may be also that each year the king took part in the renewal of covenant ceremonies at which these psalms were used. Of all the royal psalms, perhaps Psalm 72 gives the clearest description of the ideal king who was expected to bring peace and prosperity to the nation and to care for the poor and needy in his realm. These royal psalms are often interpreted Christologically (i.e. referring to the coming Messiah).

Another important group of prophecies which are taken to refer to Jesus are the Suffering Servant passages in the book of Isaiah. The most striking of these is quoted several times in the New Testament.[9] These words, for example, are referred to in the first letter of Peter in the New Testament: *But he was wounded for our transgressions, he was bruised for our iniquities; upon him was the chastisement that made us whole, and with his stripes we are healed. All we like sheep have gone astray; we have turned every one to his own way; and the Lord has laid on him the iniquity of us all.*[10] Similarly the following verses are referred to in at least one New Testament passage: *He was oppressed and he was afflicted, yet he opened not his mouth; like a lamb that is led to the slaughter, and like a sheep that before its shearer is dumb, so he opened not his mouth. By oppression and judgement he was taken away; and as for his generation, who considered that he was cut off out of the land of the living, stricken for the transgression of my people?*[11] From these and other references it is clear that the New Testament writers took the Suffering Servant passages to be prophecies about Jesus.

Another important prophecy is in the book of Daniel in the Jewish Scriptures. This is the Son of man prophecy and it has already been discussed on pages 70-71 of this book.

It seems likely that when Jesus was exploring his vocation as God's Son he considered the three types of prophecy mentioned above, that is, messianic prophecies, Suffering Servant prophecies and Son of man prophecies. He rejected the concept of kingly power while he was on earth, but Christians believe he is enthroned as King in heaven. He certainly fulfilled the Suffering Servant prophecies. As far as the Son of man prophecies are concerned, he seems to have projected this idea into the future and it is believed by some people to refer to his Second Coming. Some of the teaching which Jesus gave to his disciples refer to this future event: *...and they will see the Son of man coming on the clouds of heaven with* *power and great glory; and he will send out his angels with a loud trumpet call, and they will gather his elect from the four winds, from one end of heaven to the other.*[12] In any case, it is remarkable that so many prophecies seem to have been fulfilled in Jesus.

This is also true to some extent of prophecies about the resurrection, though not all of these refer to a particular person. A good example lies in the story of Jonah who was imprisoned for three days in the belly of a whale. Now while this may be a symbolic story, it is taken by Jesus himself to refer to his own death, entombment and resurrection. When the Pharisees ask Jesus for a sign he replies, *For as Jonah was three days and three nights in the belly of the whale, so will the Son of man be three days and three nights in the heart of the earth.*[13] In view of what happened later this is a remarkable prophecy indeed. Of course, this does not prove that the resurrection of Jesus happened, but it shows that he expected it to do so, and it also shows that Matthew believed that the prophecy came true.

Another remarkable prophecy about resurrection is recorded in the book of Ezekiel in his vision of the valley of dry bones which came to life. This is referred to in the book of Revelation, which is a Christian prophecy.[14] In the book of Daniel there is another prophecy which clearly states that the dead will rise on the Day of Judgement. The prophet writes: *And many of those who sleep in the dust of the earth shall awake, some to everlasting life, and some to shame and everlasting contempt.* The preceding verse of the Daniel passage is quoted by Jesus himself and also in the book of Revelation.[15]

There are also references in the New Testament to characters in the Jewish Scriptures who are seen as *types* who presage Jesus as priest-king or Messiah. Perhaps the best known example is King David. In the New

Testament Jesus is frequently described as being a descendant of David, and the idea of Davidic kingship as being prophetic of the coming Messiah has already been discussed. Another interesting example is that of Melchizedek, a title borrowed by David from the previous rulers of Jerusalem (Salem). The Davidic king is given the title Melchizedek in Psalm 110, a royal psalm. However, in the book of Genesis a priest-king of Salem called Melchizedek is described as presenting bread and wine to Abram, one of his vassals. In the New Testament the author of the book of Hebrews takes Melchizedek as a type for Jesus who is described as our great High Priest in heaven. The development of this idea over fifteen hundred years is remarkable. The use of bread and wine in an ancient rite is also strange when bread and wine are so important in Christianity.[16]

Moses, in renewing a covenant, also prefigured the work of Christ in a very strange way. After making a sacrifice, Moses sprinkled some of the blood onto the people and said, *Behold the blood of the covenant which the Lord has made with you in accordance with all these words.*[17] The links with Jesus' words at the Last Supper are obvious, but Paul and the author of Hebrews also make the link. Paul writes in his first letter to Corinth, when recalling the Last Supper, *This cup is the new covenant in my blood. Do this, as often as you drink it, in remembrance of me.*[18] The author of Hebrews explains the Moses passage mentioned above as prefiguring the sacrifice of Christ's blood and also sees Christ as the heavenly high priest making the sacrifice.[19]

The whole idea of covenant in the Jewish Scriptures seems to lead to the new covenant made by Christ. Take for example these words from the prophet Jeremiah in one of his few optimistic predictions: *Behold, the days are coming, says the Lord, when I will make a new covenant with the house of Israel and the house of Judah, not like the covenant which I made with their fathers...*[20] These words also are strongly echoed by the words of Jesus at the Last Supper.

The Annunciation to the Blessed Virgin Mary is also prefigured in the Jewish Scriptures. There are several examples where people are told beforehand that they are going to have a child. In other words they have annunciations from angels or from the Spirit of God. A good example lies in the story of Abraham and Sarah, who were told by three visitors to their tent that Sarah would bear a child, despite the fact hat she was beyond the usual age for child bearing.[21] Similarly, the wife of Manoah the Danite had an annunciation: *And the angel of the Lord appeared to the woman and said to her, 'Behold, you are barren and have no children; but you shall conceive and bear a son.'*[22] Additionally, of course, there is the Immanuel sign given to King Ahaz by Isaiah, already discussed above.[23]

The theology of the Jewish Scriptures presents many ideas which are developed in the New Testament. It would be no exaggeration to say that the New Testament could not have been written without some understanding of the Jewish Scriptures. It is also true that the Incarnation would not have been understood fully without the benefit of primary Jewish ideas. Take, for example, the idea of atonement. The people of the Jewish Scriptures actually had a Day of Atonement (still held by Jews) during which the scapegoat carried away all the sins of the nation. That practice, together with the sacrifice of the Passover Lamb, signifying freedom and redemption, helped the early Christians to comprehend the sacrifice of Christ on the cross.[24] Similarly, the exploration by the prophets and the psalmists of concepts like judgement, salvation, mercy, forgiveness, redemption and the Day of the Lord, enabled theologians like St Paul to work out a new theology.

How do we know it's all true?

It may be something of a cop-out, but it all depends what you mean by *know*. A woman might know her husband loves her, but she can't prove it scientifically. But then scientists don't always know things for certain, which is why they make hypotheses – or educated guesses if you like. Scientists also balance the weight of evidence for or against the truth of a hypothesis and may conclude that there is strong evidence in favour of the view they are putting forward. Take, for example, the efforts of scientists to understand how the universe began. One theory is referred to as the *big bang* theory. Many scientists believe it to be true, but they cannot as yet prove it. A Frenchman called Blaise Pascal who was an eighteenth-century scientist and philosopher, and who has a scientific law named after him, considered the question of whether the Christian God exists or not. He came up with a theory which is called Pascal's Wager and his argument goes something like this. If you wager that God does not exist, and live accordingly, then you risk eternal punishment in hell. Even if there is only a small possibility of going to hell, it is not worth the risk. However, if you wager that God does exist, and live accordingly, then you have everything to gain. Reason suggests that it is better to wager that God does exist.

While Pascal's argument is of interest, it is not the basis of the argument in this chapter, but it does serve to show that the results of investigation are not always clear-cut. The probability argument is a strong one, and if all the positive arguments about God's existence are taken together, then the evidence is quite strong. In the same way, if only a single prophecy is taken from the Jewish Scriptures, then the argument for the truth of the prophecy is not as strong as when all the networks of prophecies are put together. When that is done the enquirer may be led to think very carefully. Indeed, he may end up by being convinced that the main thrust of the scriptural prophecies about Christ must be true, because they add up to a logical and satisfying whole which explains some of the purposes of God.

The view from within the Christian faith is different from the perspective of the non-believer, though if an agnostic enquires seriously into prophecy and other aspects of the faith, he may become convinced of their truth. For some people their own experiences persuade them to believe in the biblical prophecies. If a person has what he believes to be foreknowledge of some event, and this belief is proved to be accurate, then he may clearly see the possibility that prophets of ancient times had similar experiences. One of the difficulties of claimed foreknowledge is that we cannot be certain of its truth until the event actually happens. We do know the outcomes of the alleged prophecies of the Bible, and in many cases the prophets lived to see their predictions come true. However, by the nature of the messianic events predicted, they obviously did not live to see them happen. Indeed, some of the prophecies claimed to be Christological were probably not intended that way by the prophets themselves. This presumably means that the Holy Spirit guided and influenced them in their prophecies, and so left a trail of secret clues which were only decipherable during and after the Incarnation.

NOTES

1 Isaiah, chapter seven, verses 10-17.
2 Ibid., chapter thirty-seven, verses 33-38.
3 Ibid., chapter forty-four, verses 24-28.
4 In Hebrew, *a young woman,* changed in the Greek version of the Jewish Scriptures to *virgin.*

5 See Isaiah, chapter seven, verse 14, and Matthew, chapter one, verses 22-23.
6 Ibid., chapter eleven, verse 2.
7 Ibid., chapter nine, verse 7.
8 See Luke, chapter four, verses 16-21; and Isaiah, chapter sixty-one, verses 1-2.
9 That is, parts of Isaiah, chapters fifty-two, verses 13-15 and chapter fifty-three.
10 Ibid., verses 5-6 and see 1 Peter, chapter two, verses 24-25.
11 Ibid., verses 7-8 and see Acts, chapter eight, verses 32-33. See also Isaiah, chapter fifty-three, verse 12 and Luke, chapter twenty-two, verse 37.
12 Matthew, chapter twenty-four, verses 30-31.
13 Ibid., chapter twelve, verse 40.
14 See Ezekiel, chapter thirty-seven; and Revelation, chapter eleven, verse 11.
15 See Daniel, chapter twelve, verses 1-2; Matthew, chapter twenty-four, verse 21; and Revelation, chapter twelve, verse 7.
16 See Genesis, chapter fourteen, verses 18-20; Psalm 110, verse 4; and Hebrews, chapter seven.
17 Exodus, chapter twenty-four, verse 8.
18 1 Corinthians, chapter eleven, verse 25.
19 Hebrews, chapter nine, verses 18-28.
20 Jeremiah, chapter thirty-one, verse 31.
21 Genesis, chapter eighteen, verses 1-15.
22 Judges, chapter thirteen, verse 3.
23 Isaiah, chapter seven, verse 14.
24 See Leviticus, chapter sixteen; and Exodus, chapter twelve.

CHAPTER TEN

Old sinners and new saints

Christianity and other religions claim to change people and the way they live. In the Jewish and Christian Bibles there is a whole network of ideas about the effect on people of a serious relationship with God. In this chapter, in order to simplify a very complex subject, five key words are discussed, first of all in the biblical context, and then in the context of life today. The five words are *Redemption*, *Forgiveness*, *Salvation*, *Reconciliation* and *Justification*. Even Christians who are familiar with these ideas find them difficult to interpret. However, an attempt will be made here to present the ideas in an uncomplicated way.

REDEMPTION

What the Bible has to say

Originally the word *redemption* (or paying a *ransom*) referred to buying freedom for slaves or prisoners, or even release from a death sentence. In ancient Jewish society a relative who took over the responsibility for a dead person's property or family was also counted as a redeemer. This involved paying a price for the property. So in the story of Ruth, Boaz was next of kin and accepted such a responsibility, including marriage to the widow, Ruth.[1]

In the story of Israel, the release of the slaves from Egypt came to be regarded as an act of redemption by God. There are many mentions of this in the Jewish Scriptures, but take for example this passage from the Book of Exodus: *I am the Lord, and I will bring you out from under the burdens of the Egyptians, and I will deliver you from their bondage, and I will redeem you with an outstretched arm and with great acts of judgement...*[2] Second Isaiah uses the same vocabulary to prophesy the release of the exiled Israelites from Babylon and their return to Jerusalem. He writes: *Break forth together into singing, you waste places of Jerusalem; for the Lord has comforted his people, he has redeemed Jerusalem.*[3]

The word *redeemer* is used in an interesting way in a famous passage in the book of Job. The author writes: *For I know that my Redeemer lives, and at last he will stand upon the earth.*[4] This is written in the context of Job's many troubles and he is relying upon divine help to vindicate him and to free him from his difficulties.

In Christian thinking each individual is in danger of being enslaved by sin, which means he is in need of redemption. Jesus is recorded as saying: *Truly, truly, I say to you, everyone who commits sin is a slave to sin.*[5] Paul builds on this thought by writing: *But thanks be to God, that you who were once slaves of sin... and having been set free from sin, have become slaves of righteousness.*[6] Paul uses the language of redemption when he tells the Corinthians that anyone called by the Lord, is *bought with a price* to be *a freedman of the Lord.*[7] The price, of course, was the sacrifice of Christ upon the cross. Jesus himself makes this clear when he says: *...the Son of man came not to be served but to serve, and to give his life as a ransom for many.*[8] According to Luke, the old priest, Zechariah, prophesied that this was the vocation of Jesus, as written in the

Benedictus: *Blessed be the Lord God of Israel, for he has visited and redeemed his people, and has raised up a horn of salvation for us in the house of his servant David...*[9]

What does it mean for me?

People are more familiar with the word *freedom* than with the word *redemption*, though people still use the vocabulary of redemption in some contexts. For example, goods which have been pawned may be *redeemed* at a price. The word *redeem* is also used of paying off a loan or a promissory note, or of receiving goods or money for trading stamps. However, some people go through life with out ever using the word *redeem*. This makes it more difficult to communicate this aspect of Christian thinking.

It is probably easier to start by talking about release from ills of various kinds. People can be captive to all sorts of things. Addiction to drugs is a form of imprisonment, as indeed, is addiction to smoking or gambling. Lack of education or poverty are also prisons and freedom is not shared equitably in these respects among the peoples of the world. Daily work can be a kind of prison in some people's eyes. Most people can understand these examples readily enough. But what of the biblical idea of being imprisoned by sin? In any case, what is sin? In one respect sin could be defined as falling short of ideals, but if someone has no ideals – though this must surely be rare – then that definition is not too helpful. However, perhaps most people can understand what selfishness means and that is certainly relevant to what people mean by sin. People who judge that other people are selfish must, in fact, have an ideal of sorts, that is, of unselfishness. Presumably they try to be unselfish themselves, but don't always succeed. In other words, they are prisoners of their own raw human nature.

They may well feel regret at times for the selfish way they have behaved. This is similar to the religious idea of repentance, when a people are aware of sorrow for wrong things they believe they have done – or even for right things they know they have not done.

To be redeemed, then, is to attain freedom, but in the religious sense what does freedom mean? Essentially it is freedom to grow spiritually to be a whole person. This does include the traditional Christian view of redemption from sin, but that redemption is not a once-and-for-all event, because sadly the repentant sinner falls into sin again. However, the process allows freedom from guilt (provided attempts are made at restitution) and freedom to make a new start. This is a process of growth and involves a continuing relationship with Christ. Some churches formalise this relationship in a system of penitence, confession, penance and absolution. Other churches leave it to the individual's conscience and his direct personal relationship with God. However, no system will work unless the wish to make a new start is genuine. Nevertheless, systems do help people in this process.

FORGIVENESS

As already indicated, forgiveness for past wrongs is a central part of the Christian faith. This idea needs to be discussed in more detail in order to understand it more clearly.

What the Bible has to say

The Jewish Scriptures emphasise in a number of places that God has a forgiving nature. Some of the psalms make this point plainly. For example Psalm 130 reads: *If thou, O Lord, shouldst mark iniquities, Lord, who could stand? But there is forgiveness with thee, that thou mayst be feared.*[10] The prophets also write of God's forgiveness. The book of Isaiah reads: *I am He who blots out your transgressions for my own sake, and I will not remember your sins.*[11] Similarly, Jeremiah writes: *...for they shall all know me... for I will remember their sin no more.*[12] Of course, these statements about forgiveness have to be seen in the context of God's judgement. A fascinating passage in the book of Exodus describes what God is like, but gives a warning: *The Lord, the Lord, a God merciful and gracious, slow to anger, and abounding in steadfast love and faithfulness, keeping steadfast love for thousands, forgiving iniquity and transgression and sin, but who will by no means clear the guilty...*[13] The *guilty*, presumably, are those who refuse to repent. The passage goes on to point out that the effects of their sin will continue through their descendants.

In the New Testament also there is a clear picture of a forgiving God. In the first letter of John is written: *If we confess our sins, he is faithful and just, and will forgive our sins and cleanse us from all unrighteousness.*[14] St Paul speaks of forgiveness through Christ in a sermon at Antioch: *Let it be known to you therefore, brethren, that through this man (Jesus) forgiveness of sins is proclaimed to you...*[15] However, repentance is necessary before forgiveness can take place, for otherwise the person is not in a fit state to receive forgiveness. John the Baptist, for example, is recorded as *preaching a baptism of repentance for the forgiveness of sins.*[16] After Pentecost Peter preaches a similar message. He says, *Repent, and be baptised every one of you in the name of Jesus Christ for the forgiveness of your sins...*[17]

There is much to be learned about forgiveness from the actions and words of Jesus. There are the unforgettable words on the cross when he said, *Father, forgive them; for they know not what they do.*[18] To pray for forgiveness for his murderers in those circumstances is, by human standards, astonishing; and it is perfectly true of course that those who crucified him were ignorant of his true identity. Then there is the most famous prayer of all time, that is, the Lord's prayer, in which Jesus taught his disciples in all ages to say: *Forgive us our debts (or trespasses), as we also have forgiven our debtors.*[19] Moreover, being the excellent teacher that he was, Jesus told a number of stories to emphasise the need for us to forgive as we are forgiven. There is the parable about the man who is relieved from a debt by his king, but then goes and does the opposite to someone who owes him money, putting him in prison. The king hears of this and is wrathful, placing the ungrateful servant in prison until he has paid his debt. Jesus ends the story with these words: *So also my heavenly Father will do to every one of you, if you do not forgive your brother from your heart.*[20] St Paul takes up the same theme when he writes to the church at Ephesus: *...be kind to one another, tender hearted, forgiving one another, as God in Christ forgave you.*[21]

Jesus astonished and offended his earthly contemporaries by publicly forgiving people's sins. Mark records a story about the healing of a paralysed man to whom Jesus says, before healing him, *My son, your sins are forgiven.* The scribes are outraged because they feel that only God should forgive sins. Jesus knows their thoughts and says, *Which is easier, to say to the paralytic, 'Your sins are forgiven' or to say, 'Rise, take up your pallet and walk.'*[22] Jesus then promptly cures the man. In John's Gospel there is the famous story about the woman who has committed adultery. After asking the accusers to cast the first stone if they are innocent, he then tells the woman to sin no more, and instead of being stoned she goes her way.[23] Another wonderful example of such direct forgiveness is in the story of the sinful woman who anointed Jesus' feet with costly ointment. Jesus explains that those who are forgiven many sins will give much love in return, whereas those who are forgiven little will only love a little.[24]

The idea of atonement is closely connected with the process of forgiveness. The Jewish Day of Atonement and its influence on Christian thinking has already been mentioned in chapter nine. The English word *atonement* literally means *at-one-ment*. The Hebrew word (*kaphar*) originally meant *to cover*, which came to mean that a person's sins were covered or forgiven. An equivalent word used in the Greek New Testament (*katallasso*) means to reconcile which, of course, means to bring people together, or figuratively to make them one, or of one mind. This word is used of God's relationship to people, especially by St Paul. In his letter to the Romans Paul writes: *...but we also rejoice in God through our Lord Jesus Christ, through whom we have now received our reconciliation.* In his argument he goes on to say: *...one man's (Christ's) act of righteousness leads to acquittal and life for all men.* So, Paul argues, through the atoning work of Christ on the cross, grace comes to sinners and they are made righteous.[25]

A number of passages in the New Testament make clear that forgiveness comes through the sacrificial blood of Christ. Paul makes this point: *In him we have redemption through his blood, the forgiveness of our trespasses, according to the riches of his grace which he lavished upon us.*[26] Jesus himself proclaims in hallowed words that one of the purposes of his sacrifice on the cross is forgiveness: *Drink of it, all of you; for this is my blood of the covenant, which is poured out for many for the forgiveness of sins.*[27]

To understand this idea fully it is necessary to turn back yet again to the Jewish Day of Atonement in ancient times. Even a cursory reading of the instructions for this festival in the book of Leviticus shows that blood is important in the ceremony. The blood of a sacrifice is sprinkled on the altar and on the mercy seat. The latter was a golden shelf on top of the Ark of the Covenant. The Hebrew word for mercy seat is from the same root as the word for atonement, and a literal translation would be to call the object a *cover* for the ark; and as already pointed out, sins are *covered* or forgiven in the atonement rite. To make doubly sure of forgiveness for the nation, the high priest confessed the nation's sins with his hands on the scapegoat, which was then released in the wilderness, taking the sins of the nation with it. In other words, the goat acted as a substitute. One theory of how the atonement on the cross works is called substitution, the idea being that Jesus puts himself in our place and accepts the punishment we deserve for our sins. Another theory suggests that Jesus was representative of all humanity. These theories lead to the thought that God himself accepts the retribution that sin deserves, so freeing us and forgiving us. The lesson for all of us is that forgiveness can be painful, that to withhold the punishment of the offender may be to take the punishment upon ourselves.

What forgiveness means for me

Forgiving is one aspect of loving. An understanding of people's motives and reasons helps us to forgive, for then we realise that in similar circumstances we might behave in the same way. This is well expressed in the old proverb, *There but for the grace of God go I*. However, forgiving other people is not easy, and sometimes we are all too apt to bear grudges. One of the complications is the difficulty in trying to erase hurtful experiences from our memories, and it is not easy to forgive if we can't forget.

Another complication is that we remember the ways in which we ourselves have hurt other people. How can we accept God's forgiveness if we still remember what we have done wrong? The conscience can sometimes stab like a knife. Well, we have to learn to forgive ourselves, just as we have to try to forgive others. It is very destructive to allow our own sins to fester in our minds for years.

Whichever way we look at it, the road to forgiveness is steep. However, constant prayer for God's help and grace are vital to the learning process. What we are learning is to try to love others as Christ loved us; and to recognise that his self sacrifice on the cross was for each one of us. In the broader perspective, learning to forgive and be forgiven is part of the overall process of learning to love and to be loved. This in turn is part of the life process of preparation for eternal life with Christ.

However, along with learning forgiveness there is the need to grow as an individual, and sometimes a stand against other people's behaviour is the right approach in particular circumstances. This aspect of our characters is important. We need to develop into strong minded and independent people. The person who breaks the social rules flagrantly, and without care for other people, needs to learn also that forgiveness from the people around him depends on his making amends. In the same way, if we ourselves continue to be selfish or to hurt other people, we may have to learn hard lessons before God will accept us in love and forgive us. Even Jesus was sometimes angry: for example, he gave the Pharisees a good dressing down[28] and also overturned the tables of the money-changers in the temple.[29] At the same time we need to distinguish between that kind of righteous anger and vindictive pettiness. It is of little spiritual value to allow resentment to poison one's own mind. Moreover, anger is more justified on other people's behalf than on our own. Protection of the persecuted or of those who suffer injustice is surely a Christian duty.

The wrong things a few people do may seem to most people to be very wicked. What do we do about those who seem to us to be beyond the moral pale? Well, to some extent it up to the people who have actually been hurt. However, it may be that some sins are so serious that perhaps we have no right to forgive the people who have committed them. It may be that only God has the right to do that. What we can do is pray about the situation, whatever it may be, and to commend the victims into God's care. As to the perpetrators, we may well commend them to God's judgement.

SALVATION

What the Bible has to say

Much of the Bible is about God saving man in some way, so it would be unrealistic to try to cover every aspect of the subject in a few paragraphs. Consequently, only a few of the main themes are discussed.

One of the most important aspects of salvation in the Bible is the name *Jesus*, which is derived from the Jewish word for salvation, *yeshu'ah,* which is also the origin of the name *Joshua*. In the story of the Annunciation in Luke's Gospel, Gabriel instructs Mary that she should call the son she is to bear *Jesus*.[30] In Matthew's Gospel it is recorded that the Lord tells Joseph to call the baby *Jesus, for he will save his people from their sins*.[31] Beyond the death and resurrection of Jesus, his name became very important in prayer. For example, after the Day of Pentecost, Peter says in his sermon before the Jewish court: *And there is salvation in no one else, for there is no other name under heaven given among men by which we must saved.*[32]

The salvation given by Jesus is potentially universal, *potentially* because men have the freewill to refuse the saving power of Christ. Timothy writes: *This is good and acceptable in the sight of God our Saviour, who desires all men to be saved... for there is one God, and there is one mediator between God and men, the man Jesus Christ who gave himself as a ransom for all...*[33] On a similar theme, John writes in one of his letters: *And we have seen and testify that the Father has sent his Son as the Saviour of the world.*[34]

Of course, the idea of God as Saviour has a long history, as recorded in the Jewish Scriptures. For example, in the book of Isaiah the prophet says: *And there is no other God besides me, a righteous God and a Saviour.*[35] The psalmists mention the idea of God's salvation frequently. In one psalm we read: *The Lord is my light and my salvation; whom shall I fear?*[36] This could be interpreted spiritually or in the physical sense. A good example of the expectation of practical help is recorded in the second book of Kings. The prophet Isaiah speaks God's word to the worried king: *For I will defend this city, to save it, for my own sake and for the sake of my servant David.*[37] There is a wonderful example of physical help in the book of Daniel. When three Jewish friends are to be placed in a white hot furnace they are confident of God's saving help. They say to Nebuchadnezzar: *...our God whom we serve is able to deliver us from the burning fiery furnace...*[38] An example of expectation of spiritual help is recorded by a psalmist who writes: *Deliver me from all my transgressions.*[39]

It would be inaccurate to say that there was a development from the idea of practical help to spiritual help. In both the Jewish Scriptures (as seen above) and in the New Testament, both ideas exist side by side. In the New Testament, alongside the many promises of spiritual salvation, there are a number of examples of God saving people in dire circumstances. For example, Peter is released from prison by an angel sent by God.[40]

Paul had similar experiences. When he is in danger of shipwreck, an angel speaks to him in a vision: *Do not be afraid, Paul; you must stand before Caesar; and lo, God has granted you all those who sail with you.*[41] A very specific example of spiritual salvation is mentioned by Peter: *As the outcome of your faith you obtain the salvation of your souls.*[42]

St Paul notes that it is through the Gospel that we are saved: *Now I would remind you, brethren, in what terms I preached to you the gospel, which you received, in which you stand, by which you are saved, if you hold it fast – unless you believed in vain.*[43] Of course, strictly speaking, it is not the Gospel that saves, though it does lead the believer to the Saviour, that is, to Jesus. Faith in the power of Jesus to save is, however, a factor in the equation. As Paul says to the worried jailer at Philippi; *Believe in the Lord Jesus, and you will be saved, you and your household.*[44] Paul clarifies this further, however, in one of his letters: *For by grace you have been saved through faith; and this is not your own doing, it is the gift of God – not because of works...*[45] Much has been made in some church circles of this idea that salvation cannot be earned by man himself, but that it is God's free gift. In a later and very beautiful passage of his letter to Ephesus, Paul describes how God's armour may help us to withstand against the attacks of the world, the flesh and the devil.[46] To Paul, God's saving power was very real in every way.

There is a great dramatic irony in one passage which describes Jesus speaking to Andrew and Philip, two of his close disciples. He explains that the Son of man, like an apparently dead grain of wheat, must die and be glorified. However, Jesus' humanity makes him sad and apprehensive at the thought. He says to them: *Now is my soul troubled. And what shall I say? 'Father save me from this hour'? No, for this purpose I have come to this hour. Father, glorify thy name.*[47] The irony is that Jesus is the Saviour of mankind, but he feels like praying to be saved himself, though he rejects the thought. Another example of dramatic irony occurs while Jesus is being crucified. The scribes and Pharisees mock him, saying, *He saved others; he cannot save himself.*[48] Little do they know that Jesus is, in fact, the Saviour of the world.

One result of the Saviour's death and resurrection is that Christians believe that they too take part in the resurrection. Although belief in the resurrection appeared in Jewish thought in the work of prophets like Ezekiel and Daniel, the idea of saving from death, for example in the psalms, is ambiguous. It often seems to mean that the one saved is allowed to continue his life in this world. Sometimes it seems to be a piece of poetic symbolism. Take this passage from Psalm 18: *The cords of death encompassed me, the torrents of perdition assailed me; the cords of Sheol entangled me, the snares of death confronted me. In my distress I called upon the Lord; to my God I cried for help. From his temple he heard my voice, and my cry to him reached his ears.*[49] This is typical of many statements about God saving from death in the Jewish Scriptures. However, what is probably the best-known psalm in the collection, the 23rd Psalm, seems in the traditional translation to promise life after death and the comfort of God for those passing on. The Revised Standard Version of the Bible reads: *Even though I walk through the valley of the shadow of death, I fear no evil; for thou art with me...*[50] Many people have found comfort in these words, but the translation is by no means certain. It would be equally valid to translate: *...the valley of deep darkness...* as a footnote in RSV points out.

In the New Testament, on the other hand, a new dimension appears – because of the central belief in the resurrection of Jesus. In a letter to Timothy, for example,

Paul writes: ...*through the appearing of our Saviour Christ Jesus, who abolished death and brought light and immortality to light through the gospel.*[51] James ends his letter with a revealing statement: ...*whoever brings back a sinner from the error of his way will save his soul from death and will cover a multitude of sins.*[52] Of course, the New Testament contains frequent references both to the resurrection of Jesus and to the resurrection of the believer.

What does being *saved* mean?

As has been pointed out in the biblical examples, a person may be saved by God in a practical and literal sense, and this is just as true today as it was in biblical times. In fact, many people who do not profess religion in any formal sense, still pray for help when they are in danger or trouble. Many people testify to being saved from danger by prayer. Unfortunately, it seems that some people pray for help and are not heard. Even when the danger passes, it is difficult to know whether God has intervened, or whether the danger would have passed anyway. It is a matter of faith and belief in the power of God. In cases where he does not intervene with help, we have to assume that from God's perspective, for whatever reason, it is better not to intervene. Take for example three people, Albert, Brian and Colin, who are diagnosed as having cancer. All three pray for a cure that will save their lives. Albert is cured and accepts that he has had God's help. Brian is cured but eventually concludes that it was the doctor who cured him and that God had nothing to do with it. Colin, however, is not cured and he dies. Why has God not answered Colin's prayer? This problem is difficult to penctrate, but it may be that it is time for Colin to move on because he is ready for the real life beyond death; and there is a need for him to continue there, rather than here.

But what of salvation in the spiritual sense? To a large extent this question has already been answered in the discussion of redemption earlier in the chapter. To be *redeemed* or *freed* from sin is similar to being *saved* from sin, and that is a continuing process. One important point, however, is that the idea of being saved is connected with the name of Jesus as Saviour. Of course, it is true that he is also called Redeemer, but there is a distinct difference. In prayer it is more natural to say *Save me, Lord!* than it is to say *Redeem me, Lord!*

In some churches there is a great emphasis on being *saved*. This is usually seen as a once-and-for-all-action by God in relation to an individual. However, the evidence suggests that when a person is *saved* in that sense, he or she is only at the beginning of an ongoing spiritual development. In other words, they are still not perfect, though they may be aware that their sins are forgiven.

On the question of resurrection, if we do survive after death, and it is Christian teaching that we do, then it is probably the case that there always has been a life after death, even before the revelation through Christ. What the Gospel does is reveal with certainty what had been hidden since man first appeared in the world – that there is another stage of life after this one.

RECONCILIATION

What the Bible has to say

Jesus himself gives an important message about reconciliation between people who have quarrelled. In his famous Sermon on the Mount, he explains that if you have had a disagreement with someone, and you remember this as you approach God's altar with a gift, what you ought to do before presenting your gift is to be reconciled with your brother. Jesus goes on to say:

Make friends quickly with your accuser, while you are going with him to court, lest your accuser hand you over to the judge...and you be put in prison.[53] This means that we cannot be at peace with God if we are at odds with our neighbour.

Reconciliation with God is a different matter. St Paul has strong opinions about this. In his letter to Rome he shows that it is through the death of Christ on the cross that we are *justified by his blood*. In this context, *justified* means to be made righteous (a concept which is discussed in the next section of this chapter). This saves us from God's wrath, and through this process we are reconciled with God. Now to speak of reconciliation with someone implies that there has been a division between them. In this case, the division was (and is) caused by human sinfulness. While much sin is an offence against our neighbour, all sin is an offence against God. This is so because God's perfect righteousness and holiness finds human unrighteous and unholiness incompatible with His character. But the incompatible is made compatible by God's own action. Those who accept God's grace are able to approach God as new beings. However, as already pointed out, this process is a continuous one, because we keep falling from grace again and again. Prayer is the main means by which God's grace is continually renewed.[54]

In his second letter to Corinth, Paul associates reconciliation with the new creation of the self that those in Christ experience. Through Christ we are given *the ministry of reconciliation, that is, in Christ God was reconciling the world to himself, not counting their trespasses against them, and entrusting to us the message of reconciliation.* This means that every Christian who has received God's grace and has become reconciled to Him, has the responsibility of giving the message to the world, or at any rate to those around him or her.[55]

In his letter to Ephesus, Paul again takes up the subject of reconciliation, this time in relation to non-Jews. He explains that they were once without citizenship in the nation of Israel, but that now, through the blood of Christ, they have been made one with the citizens of the new Israel. In other words, Gentiles and Jews, who were once at enmity with each other, are united in the Church of Christ. *He (Christ) is our peace, who has made us both one, and has broken down the dividing wall of hostility, by abolishing in his flesh the law of commandments and ordinances, that he might create in himself one new man in place of the two, so making peace, and might reconcile us both to God in one body through the cross, thereby bringing the hostility to an end.* The importance of this message is that when Christians are for any reason in disagreement with each other, Christ has the capacity to reconcile them, if only they will turn their hearts and minds to him.[56]

In his letter to Colossae, Paul again writes of reconciliation. Yet again he emphasises that it is the blood of the cross which brings reconciliation with God, that those who were estranged from God are now one with him. Paul sees this process as universal. Through Christ, God was able *to reconcile to himself all things, whether on earth or in heaven...* Further, this reconciliation exists with a condition – *that you continue in the faith, stable and steadfast, not shifting from the hope of the gospel...* This means that if a man falls away from the faith he will revert to his former condition of being at hostility with God.[57]

What this means to me

In the hurly-burly of every day it is not always easy to set the mind on reconciliation with God. Nor is it easy to pursue reconciliation with those from whom we have become estranged. This is why it is so important to set aside some time for prayer and serious thought, even if it is only for a few minutes. Ideally, such quiet periods could take place both morning and evening, but many people are in too much of a rush in the morning. However, the evening time is perhaps more important for reviewing the events of the day that is past, together with the state of our relationships with those around us.

Reconciliation with God is, as we have seen, connected with reconciliation with people. If we are bearing grudges or wishing ill fortune upon someone, then we are not going to be in a suitable mental or spiritual state to make our peace with God. So if a man is at odds with his neighbour, who is to make the first move? There is the danger of rejection, of course, which might make the hostility even worse. A small diplomatic move might be advisable, but then every one is different and situations are different, so it is difficult to set up rules. However, tentative advice might go something like this. Pray about the situation first. Whatever we do, do with Christian love in our hearts. Be mentally prepared for either a friendly or hostile reaction and have an appropriately loving answer ready. Whatever the result, pray again and offer the situation to God. Above all, try to excise any resentment from our minds and try to stay close to God.

Unfortunately, some hostile situations seem impossible to resolve. So what do we do when we approach God to be reconciled with him? It is clear that we cannot deceive God, so we must lay the situation before him and ask for help. If in all conscience we have done what we can to right any wrongs, then we can pray God's blessing upon the person who is at odds with us, and pray for a resolution to the problem at some time in the future.

The teaching of Jesus on how to deal with our enemies is clear, but difficult to put into practice. In the Sermon on the Mount he says, *But I say to you, Love your enemies and pray for those who persecute you, so that you may be sons of your Father who is in heaven...*[58] This amounts to a serious attempt to be reconciled with both God and man.

JUSTIFICATION

What the Bible has to say

In the Jewish Scriptures the word used for *justification*, and associated words, have a whole range of meanings. There are associations with the law courts in that the word is used to show someone can be *proved to be upright* or can be *declared innocent*. This means to say that they can be justified legally. However, the word can also mean to be just in one's dealings. The noun, also with several meanings, can mean *salvation* or *well being*. These expressions have echoes in the New Testament, as will be seen below.

The book of Job gives a good example of the legal aspect. Job, who is accused of wrongdoing, claims that he has prepared his case and knows that he can be vindicated (justified). This of course is in an imaginary court of law. Job is speaking of being proved righteous before God.[59] A similar use of the word is shown in a long prayer in which King Solomon asks God to condemn the guilty and to vindicate (justify) the righteous, implying that human behaviour is judged by God as if in a court of law.[60]

One of the psalms concludes, however, that no man can be justified before God. The psalmist writes, *Enter not into judgement with thy servant, for no man living is righteous before thee.*[61] St Paul, who may of course have been influenced by the psalm, has a similar thought: *For no human being will be justified in his sight by works of the law, since through the law comes knowledge of sin.*[62]

One of the deepest thinkers on this subject in the Jewish Scriptures is the prophet known as Second Isaiah, taken to be the author of Isaiah 40-55. He writes a number of poems about a suffering servant who sometimes seems to be an individual, though at other times seems to be the whole nation of Israel. In one passage the servant is described as being put to shame. As if in a law court the servant says, *...he who vindicates me is near.... Who is my adversary? Let him come near to me. Behold, the Lord God helps me; who will declare me guilty?*[63] In the best known suffering servant poem, the author explains that the servant, through his suffering, *when he makes himself an offering for sin... will ...make many to be accounted righteous, and he shall bear their iniquities.*[64] This description is so much a parallel with Christ's suffering and atoning work, that it must surely be interpreted as a prophecy of Christ's great work in the incarnation.

The inter-connected words used on this subject in the New Testament are also connected with the law courts. Originally the word *justify* meant *judge* in the form of punishment, but in the New Testament it means *save* in the sense of *acquittal*. Jesus uses the expression in one of his parables. He describes a Pharisee and a tax collector, showing how the former is self righteous, whereas the latter is very conscious of his sin. Jesus says that the tax collector is justified (made righteous) more than the other.

St Paul uses this terminology more than any other New Testament writer. Indeed, it is well known that Paul has a theology of justification by faith and grace, rather than by good works. In his letter to Rome he especially emphasises this doctrine. He writes: *...since all have sinned and fall short of the glory of God, they are justified by his grace as a gift, through the redemption which is in Christ Jesus. whom God put forward as an expiation by* *his blood, to be received by faith.*[65] By contrast, no one will be justified by works of the law, *since through the law comes knowledge of sin.*[66] It is also well known that James, in his letter, opposes this doctrine. He writes: *But someone will say, 'You have faith and I have works.' Show me your faith apart from your works, and I by my works will show you my faith. ...You see that a man is justified by works and not by faith alone.*[67]

It is ironic that both Paul and James use the patriarch Abraham to support their argument. James argues that because Abraham offered Isaac on the altar, though he was not required to carry out the sacrifice, he was justified by his action, fulfilling his faith as shown when the Genesis author writes: *Abraham believed God and it was reckoned to him as righteousness.*[68] By contrast, Paul uses this very same quotation to argue that Abraham was justified only by his faith. Paul then goes on to write: *So also David pronounces a blessing upon the man to whom God reckons righteous apart from works.*[69] This serves to show how difficult biblical interpretation can be. It is the present author's view that God's grace and good works go hand in hand. Someone receiving God's grace will try to do good: someone who tries to do good, will receive God's grace.

Paul makes several other points about justification. With reference to Jews and Gentiles he writes: *...he (God) will justify the circumcised on the ground of their faith and the uncircumcised through their faith.*[70] This means that neither group has superiority over the other. He also writes in his first letter to Corinth: *But you were washed, you were sanctified, you were justified in the name of the Lord Jesus Christ and in the Spirit of our God.*[71] This thought is clarified by his comment in Romans on the saving work of Christ: *But God shows his love for us in that while we were yet sinners Christ died for us. Since, therefore, we are now justified by his* *blood, much more shall we be saved by him from the wrath of God.*[72]

What this means to me

In every day life we tend to use the word *justify* in a rather different context from the biblical one. For example, we say that a person's actions may be justified by the result of what he has done. Someone, who is at first criticised as a nuisance by the media for organising a public protest, may succeed in his aim of getting farmers a better deal. Some of the media may then say that the man was justified. The similarity with the biblical meaning is there. The man has been declared right: he has been acquitted at the bar of media opinion. In a similar way God acquits us at the bar of judgement and we are justified or declared righteous. This means that we can make a new start with a clean sheet.

Another example from life is the idea of the just war. When is a nation justified in going to war? Various criteria have been put forward over the centuries by people as prominent as Thomas Aquinas. For example, it is said that the war must have a just reason behind it and that the intention must be to do good. This, of course, has a religious aspect, in that the participants in a so-called just war hope that they will be justified in their actions before God.

In the spiritual context, as we have seen in previous sections, the justification by God's grace is the wiping away of past sins achieved by the work of Christ on the cross. We stand at the bar of God's judgement. Inevitably, because we fall short of perfection, we are guilty. However, Christ stands at the judgement seat alongside us and intercedes for us. In effect, the Son is saying to the Father, "Look, I have accepted the punishment for these people, so will you give them a new start, starting from square one." The paradox is that the Father and the Son are One, so it is God who is judging us, but at the same time justifying us, or making us right with him. This, indeed, is a gift of wonderful grace.

NOTES

---

1. Ruth, chapter three, verse 9; chapter four, verses 4-6 and 14-15.
2. Exodus, chapter six, verse 6.
3. Isaiah, chapter fifty-two, verse 9.
4. Job, chapter nineteen, verse 25.
5. John, chapter eight, verse 34.
6. Romans, chapter six, verses 17-18.
7. 1 Corinthians, chapter seven, verses 22-24.
8. Matthew, chapter twenty, verse 28.
9. Luke, chapter one, verses 68-69.
10. Psalm 130, verses 3-4.
11. Isaiah, chapter forty-three, verses 25.
12. Jeremiah, chapter thirty-one, verse 34.
13. Exodus, chapter thirty-four, verses 6-7.
14. 1 John, chapter one, verse 9.
15. Acts, chapter thirteen, verse 38.
16. Mark, chapter one, verse 4.
17. Acts, chapter two, verse 38.
18. Luke, chapter twenty-three, verse 34.
19. Matthew, chapter six, verse 12; and cf. verse 15.
20. Ibid., chapter eighteen, verses 23-35.
21. Ephesians, chapter four, verse 32.
22. Mark, chapter two, verses 1-14.
23. It is disputed as to whether or not this story has been added to the original of John's Gospel. See John's Gospel, chapter eight, verses 2-11.
24. Luke, chapter seven, verses 36-50.
25. See Romans, chapter five, verses 6-21.
26. Ephesians, chapter one, verses 7-8.
27. Matthew, chapter twenty-six, verse 28.
28. See Matthew, chapter twenty-three.
29. See Mark, chapter eleven, verses 15-19.
30. Luke, chapter one, verses 26-31.
31. Matthew, chapter one, verses 18-23.

32 Acts, chapter four, verse 12.
33 1 Timothy, chapter two, verses 3-6.
34 1 John, chapter four, verse 14.
35 Isaiah, chapter forty-five, verse 21.
36 Psalm 27, verse 1.
37 2 Kings, chapter nineteen, verse 34.
38 Daniel, chapter three, verse 17. It is a matter of interpretation as to whether or not this story is to be taken symbolically or interpreted literally.
39 Psalm 39, verse 8.
40 See Acts, chapter twelve, verses 1-17.
41 Ibid., chapter twenty-seven, verses 21-26.
42 1 Peter, chapter one, verse 9.
43 1 Corinthians, chapter fifteen, verses 1-2.
44 Acts, chapter sixteen, verse 31.
45 Ephesians, chapter two, verse 8-9.
46 Ibid., chapter six, verses 10-20.
47 John, chapter twelve, verse 27.
48 Mark, chapter fifteen, verse 31.
49 Psalm 18, verses 4-6.
50 Psalm 23, verse 4.
51 2 Timothy, chapter one, verse 10.
52 James, chapter five, verse 20.
53 See Matthew, chapter five, verses 21-26.
54 See Romans, chapter five, verses 6-11.
55 See 2 Corinthians, chapter five, verses 16-19.
56 See Ephesians, chapter two, verses 11-22.
57 See Colossians, chapter one, verses 19-23.
58 Matthew, chapter five, verses 44-45.
59 Job, chapter thirteen, verse 18.
60 1 Kings, chapter eight, verse 32.
61 Psalm 143, verse 2.
62 Romans, chapter three, verse 20.
63 Isaiah, chapter fifty, verses 8-9.
64 Ibid., chapter fifty-three, verses 10-11.
65 Romans, chapter three, verses 23-25 and see verse 28.
66 Ibid., verse 20; and cf. Galatians, chapter two, verse 16 and chapter three, verse 11.
67 James, chapter two, verses 18 and 24.
68 See Genesis, chapter fifteen, verse 6.
69 See Romans, chapter four, verses 1-8; and cf. Galatians, chapter three, verse 8.
70 Ibid., chapter three, verse 30.
71 1 Corinthians, chapter six, verse 11.
72 Romans, chapter five, verses 8-9.

CHAPTER ELEVEN

Unbroken chain

If God has revealed himself over a long period of history, what was the starting point of his action, at least from our limited human perspective? If the Judaeo-Christian tradition is taken as a time line with a beginning, then possibly the call of the patriarch Abram is a realistic place to start a historical account. However, that is not quite what the Bible does, for the biblical compilers start with creation and follow with stories of mythical figures like Noah. It is true that some people might argue that Noah was a historical figure, but bearing in mind that a similar Babylonian myth survives, it is almost impossible to find convincing historical data about Noah and other characters supposedly living before the time of Abraham. This is not to say that the stories are of no value. In fact they illustrate deep spiritual truths. The story of the fall of Adam and Eve, for example, expresses a truth about human nature.

Although some people might argue that Abram also was a mythical figure, many commentators have concluded that he existed historically as a tribal leader. It is true that the stories about him have been edited from oral traditions, but the Jewish traditions about Abram are so strong that it is difficult to discard the stories as fiction. Supposing, then, that Abram lived around 1750 BC, then it seems perfectly possible that he was called by God to found a nation. According to the story, God promised that Abram would be the father of many people; *Then Abram fell on his face; and God said to him, 'Behold, my covenant is with you, and you shall be the father of a multitude of nations.*[1] The amazing thing is that now, after almost four thousand years, millions of Jews, Christians and Muslims regard Abram (also called Abraham) as the spiritual founding father of their religion.

The story of Abraham leads to other patriarchal stories about Isaac, Jacob and his twelve sons, and culminates in a period in Egypt, first as guests and then as slaves. During this period of slavery Moses appears as a towering figure who creates Israel as a nation. Not only does he lead the slaves out of Egypt, he also formulates the well known Ten Commandments, by divine inspiration. These Commandments still guide many Jews and Christians in their daily lives. During a lengthy period of desert life Moses brings discipline and order into the lives of the Israelites, creating a system of worship with the help of Aaron, and creating a strong army which later proves to be invincible.

The next stage of development for the Chosen People was the acquisition of some land by conquest, that is, the land of Canaan. Joshua and other leaders, probably in various parts of the country, led the people up to the time of Samuel, the great kingmaker. The first king was Saul, but it was David, his successor, who founded a lasting dynasty. Although the country was divided after Solomon's day, kings reigned in Jerusalem until the sixth century BC, which was when the Babylonians conquered Judah. Up to that time, over a period of approximately five hundred years, kings, prophets and priests influenced the nation's destiny in both politics and religion. However, the prophets have been most influential in the development of the Judaeo-Christian tradition. There was an amazing succession of individuals called by God to lead the nation in its true vocation. To name but a few of the most influential prophets, the prophetic succession includes Samuel, Nathan, Elijah, Elisha, Micaiah, Isaiah, Amos, Hosea, Jeremiah and Ezekiel. These men preached God's word and were brave enough to stand up against the power of mighty kings.

Most of the influential Jews were transported to Babylon at the beginning of their exile, which lasted for fifty years or more, depending which transportation is taken as the starting point. Ezekiel and the Second Isaiah were especially influential during this time. At last, as a result of the conquests of Cyrus of Persia, some of the Chosen People returned to Jerusalem and the surrounding area. Eventually the temple was rebuilt and a new line of prophets accepted God's call. Ezra was particularly influential and founded a school of scribes who kept the scriptural tradition alive. However, Jewish development continued in Babylon and the post-biblical Jewish writings produced in Babylon were in some respects superior to those produced in Jerusalem.

Jesus of Nazareth was born into this long-standing Jewish tradition, probably a few years before the date originally assigned to his birth. As a child, he would be taught the Scriptures and customs of his people. For some years he remained in Nazareth, probably helping Joseph in the carpenter's shop. During those years he must have grown aware of his vocation and no doubt he saw himself pre-figured in scriptural prophecies. He undertook a short ministry of about three years, gathering around him twelve close disciples and other followers. He became widely known as a teacher, as a healer and as a miracle worker. He was hailed by some as the expected Messiah, but others plotted against him. This plot succeeded and Jesus was executed on a cross. Before his death he had a last supper with his twelve disciples at which he instituted the sacrament of holy communion, the broken bread symbolic of his body, and wine symbolic of his blood. Three days after his entombment the disciples saw Jesus again in several resurrection appearances.

A few weeks later Jesus made his last resurrection appearance and warned his disciples to expect the coming of the Holy Spirit. On the day of Pentecost, the Holy Spirit manifested himself to a gathering of disciples, and from that time the gospel of the risen Jesus was proclaimed. Disciples gathered into groups for worship, breaking bread and drinking wine in remembrance of Jesus, Messiah and Lord. Over several decades the Church became more organised and missionaries like St Paul spread the gospel to many countries, converting Gentiles as well as Jews. Many Christians, including St Stephen, St Peter and St Paul, were martyred for their faith. Some Roman emperors deliberately tried to stamp out Christianity. However, in the fourth century AD the Emperor Constantine became a Christian and many people throughout the empire followed his lead.

The story of Christianity from then on is very complex. Divisions appeared in the Church, for example between the Roman and the Greek Churches, and later between the Roman and the Protestant Churches. However, through all the chances and changes of history, men and women were called by God to serve Him by following Christ. Some Churches believe that there is an unbroken succession of priests and bishops from the time of St Peter, ordained by the laying on of hands. Other Churches claim that the Holy Spirit represents the true continuity of Christianity, because in each generation the Spirit has called individuals to vocations as preachers, teachers, missionaries – or to serve Christ in a host of other ways.

This continuity may best be illustrated by choosing a list of prominent Christians, one or more representing each Christian century. Each of the people listed made a significant mark on the history of Christianity.[2]

	Date[3]	**Feast day**[4]
Peter the Apostle[5]	first century	29 June
Stephen, the first Christian martyr	first century	26 Dec
John the Elder (Letters of John)	first century (John the Apostle?)	
John the Prophet (Revelation)	first century (John the Apostle?)	
Philip the Evangelist	first century	1 May
Paul, Apostle and Missionary, and Writer and Theologian	first century	25 Jan and also 29 June
James, the Lord's Brother	first century	23 Oct
Luke, Evangelist and Historian	first century	18 Oct
Ignatius of Antioch, Theologian	c. 35-c. 107	1 Feb
Clement of Rome, Pope	Active c.96	23 Nov
Polycarp, Pastor and Leader	c.69-155	26 Jan
Justin Martyr, Defender of the Faith	c. 100-165	14 Apr
Irenaeus, Theologian	c. 130-200	3 July
Clement of Alexandria, Theologian	c.150-215	5 Dec
Tertullian, Writer	c. 160-225	
Origen, Theologian	c.185-254	
Cyprian, Martyr	d. 258	16 Sept
Eusebius, Historian	c.260-340	
Constantine the Great, Emperor	(288?) 272-337	
Athanasius, Theologian	c. 296-373	2 May
Gregory of Nazianus, Theologian	329-389	9 May
Hilary of Poitiers	c. 315-67/8	13 Jan
Basil the Great, Hermit	c. 330-79	1 Jan
Ambrose, Theologian	c.339-97	4 Apr
Martin of Tours, Monk and Bishop	d. 397	11 Nov
Antony of Egypt	third/fourth century	17 Jan
Alban, Martyr	third/fourth century	17 June
Jerome, Biblical Scholar	c.345-420	30 Sept
John Chrysostom, Preacher	c. 347-407	13 Sept
Augustine of Hippo, Theologian	354-430	28 Aug
Cyril of Alexandria, Patriarch	c. 380-444	9 Feb
Leo the Great, Pope	d. 461	10 Nov
Patrick, Pastor and Leader	fifth century	17 Mar
Benedict, Monastic Founder	c. 480-550	21 Mar
Columba, Missionary	521-597	9 June
Gregory the Great, Pope	c. 540-604	3 Sept
David, Pastor and Leader	d. 601	1 Mar
Augustine of Canterbury, Archbishop	d. 604-9 (?)	26 May

Date[3]		Feast day[4]
Hilda, Abbess	614-80	17 Nov
Cuthbert, Pastor and Leader	c. 636-87	20 Mar
Aidan, Pastor and Leader	d. 651	31 Aug
Bede the Historian	c. 673-735	27 May
Boniface of Crediton, Missionary	675-754	5 June
Alcuin, Writer	c. 735-804	20 May
Photius, Patriarch	c. 810-895	6 Feb
Alfred the Great, King	849-899	26 Oct
Dunstan, Archbishop	c. 909-988	19 May
Bruno, Founder of Carthusians	1032-1101	6 Oct
Anselm, Archbishop	c. 1033-1109	21 Apr
Gregory VII, Pope	d. 1085	25 May
Bernard of Clairvaux, Abbot	1090-1153	20 Aug
Hildegard, Abbess	1098-1179	17 Sept
Bernard of Cluny, Poet	1100-1150	
Thomas Becket, Archbishop	c.1120-70	29 Dec
Innocent III, Pope	1160/1-1216	
Dominic, Founder of Dominicans	c.1172-1221	4 Aug
Francis, Founder of Franciscans	1181/2-1226	4 Oct
Clare, Abbess	1193/4-1253	11 Aug
Thomas Aquinas, Theologian	c. 1225-74	28 Jan
John Wycliffe, Theologian	c. 1330-1384	31 Dec
Julian of Norwich, Anchoress	1342-1416 (or later)	8 May
Catherine of Siena, Teacher	1347-80	29 Apr
Thomas à Kempis, Writer	1380-1471	24 July
Martin Luther, Reformer	1483-1546	
Thomas More, Martyr	1478-1535	22 June
William Tyndale, Bible Translator	1490-1536	6 Oct
Ignatius Loyola, Jesuit Founder	1491-1556	31 July
Teresa of Avila, Mystic	1515-1582	15 Oct
John Bunyan, Writer	1628-1688	31 Aug
George Fox, Quaker	1624-1691	
John Wesley, Founder Methodism	1703-1791	24 May
Nano Nagle, Teacher	1718-1784	
John Henry Newman, Cardinal	1801-1890	
David Livingstone, Missionary	1813-1873	
Albert Schweitzer, Theologian	1875-1965	
John XXIII, Pope	1881-1963	
Karl Barth, Theologian	1886-1968	
Mother Teresa, Nobel Laureate	c.1910-1997	
Oscar Romero, Martyr	1917-1980	

There are many other prominent Christians who could have been listed and, of course, there are millions of Christians unknown to us who have been links in this unbroken chain of tradition.

What of the future? In a thousand years from now will the unbroken chain still be intact? Only God knows the answer to that question. However, if it is true that God is guiding the Church of Christ through his Holy Spirit, then nothing can break the chain except an act of God. In one of his prophecies Jesus said to Peter and other disciples: *And I tell you, you are Peter*[6]*, and on this rock I will build my church, and the powers of death shall not prevail against it.*[7]

NOTES

1 Genesis, chapter seventeen, verses 3-4.
2 Any good encyclopaedia, for example the Encyclopaedia Britannica, will provide information about most of the people listed. Their stories will also be told somewhere on the Internet.
3 Many dates are approximations.
4 There may be more than one date in the calendar to celebrate a particular saint, though only one is given here.
5 A short phrase has been used to describe each person's main function in the Church but, of course, some of the people listed performed many functions.
6 The Greek word for Peter is *petros*, which means *rock*.
7 Matthew, chapter sixteen, verse 18.

CHAPTER TWELVE

The end of all things

Does life have a meaning and an ultimate destiny? Some Christian thinkers certainly put this view forward, based on biblical evidence. At the individual level, of course, there is the belief in resurrection and in continuing life in a new dimension. But what of world history? Does God have a grand plan with a climactic end? This is put forward in a doctrine called eschatology, which means *the last things*. This subject is very complex and it has led to many disputes about the Second Coming of Christ and the final judgement. The comments in this chapter barely touch the edge of the topic. However, it is too important an issue to ignore, so several related themes will be discussed briefly.

The Jewish Scriptures do have a future perspective. The messianic prophecies have already been discussed in a previous chapter, along with the son of man and suffering servant prophecies. In addition, there are several prophecies concerning the Day of the Lord, which is associated with judgement. Joel writes: *Multitudes, multitudes, in the valley of decision! For the day of the Lord is near in the valley of decision. The sun and moon are darkened, and the stars withdraw their shining.*[1] The decision mentioned is a decision of judgement. Isaiah writes of *the latter days*: *He (God) shall judge between the nations, and shall decide for many peoples; and they shall beat their swords into ploughshares, and their spears into pruning hooks; nation shall not lift up sword against nation, neither shall they learn war any more.*[2] In this idealistic prophecy Isaiah envisages an era of world peace, but as we all know this has not yet come about.

There are other prophecies which imply that God himself will come to judge the world. About *that day* Isaiah writes: *For behold, the Lord is coming forth out of his place to punish the inhabitants of the earth for their iniquity, and the earth will disclose the blood shed upon her...*[3] Zechariah writes of the day of the Lord: *And the valley of my mountains shall be stopped up, for the valley of the mountains shall touch the side of it; and you shall flee as you fled from the earthquake in the days of Uzziah king of Judah. Then the Lord your God will come, and all the holy ones with him.*[4] Many such prophecies, both in the Scriptures and in non-biblical writings, include descriptions of natural catastrophes or strange effects in the sky or supernatural revelations. The book of Daniel is an example of such apocalyptic[5] writing, and during the two centuries before Christ was born, this type of literature was quite common. In the New Testament, the book of Revelation (also called The Apocalypse) falls into this category of literature.

In fact, some of the teaching of Jesus is of the same genre. Take, for example, Mark, chapter thirteen, which is often called The Little Apocalypse. Jesus says, for instance, in the context of the last days: *But in those days, after that tribulation, the sun will be darkened, and the moon will not give its light, and the stars will be falling from heaven, and the powers in the heavens will be shaken. And then they will see the Son of man coming in clouds with great power and glory. And then he will send out the angels, and gather his elect from the four winds, from the ends of the earth to the ends of heaven.*[6] Some people today interpret these signs literally and watch out for them as a warning of the Second Coming of Christ and the end of the world (*eschaton*). Other people prefer to interpret such passages as symbolic of these events. Of course, the Second Coming of Christ may happen before and separately from the end of the world.

The Second Coming of Christ is mentioned in a number of New Testament passages. It is announced to the disciples by an angel just after the Ascension of Jesus into heaven.[7] St Paul seems to have expected Christ to come again in his (Paul's) lifetime. He writes in his first letter to Thessalonica: *For the Lord himself will descend from heaven with a cry of command, with the archangel's call, and with the sound of the trumpet of God. And the dead in Christ will rise first; then we who are alive, who are left, shall be caught up together with them in the clouds to meet the Lord.* But he also writes in the same letter: *But as to the times and seasons, brethren, you have no need to have anything written to you. For you yourselves know well that the day of the Lord will come like a thief in the night.* Moreover, he gives a warning to the church at Thessalonica in his second letter. He writes: *Now concerning the coming of our Lord Jesus Christ and our assembling to meet him, we beg you, brethren, not to be quickly shaken in mind or excited, either by spirit or by word, or by letter purporting to be from us, to the effect that the day of the Lord has come.* Paul goes on to say that Christ's coming will be preceded by a rebellion led by a lawless man who *takes his seat in the temple of God, proclaiming himself to be God...but... the Lord Jesus will slay him with the breath of his mouth and destroy him by his appearing and coming.*[8]

Other future events which may precede the Day of the Lord are described in several New Testament texts. There will be a battle between the forces of good and the forces of evil (at Armageddon); there will be great tribulation;

there will be persecution; there will be an anti-Christ or a prominent evil leader (the lawless man?); and there will be a judgement of Satan's followers.[9]

Throughout the Christian centuries up to the present day, some Christians have believed in a doctrine called Millenarianism. This is based on a passage in the book of Revelation which states: *Also I saw the souls of those who had been beheaded for their testimony to Jesus... They came to life and reigned with Christ a thousand years.* On a similar line, St Paul writes: *Then comes the end, when he delivers the kingdom to God the Father after destroying every rule and every authority and power. For he must reign until he has put all his enemies under his feet.*[10] Opinion is divided among believers in Millenarianism as to whether the thousand years precedes or follows the Second Coming of Christ. Those who believe in the former, take the period as a time of preparation for Christ's Coming during which there will be a growth in righteousness throughout the world.[11]

Jesus' own view of the kingdom of God (or the kingdom of heaven) seems to be ambiguous. Sometimes he teaches that it is here and now. At other times he teaches that it will come in the future. Of course, there are many references to the kingdom in the teaching of Jesus. However to illustrate the point, the following examples are taken. On the one hand he says, *The kingdom of God is not coming with signs to be observed; nor will they say, 'Lo, here it is!' or 'There!' for behold, the kingdom of God is in the midst of you.*[12] This proclaims that the kingdom is a present reality. On the other hand he says, *Truly, I say to you, there are some standing here who will not taste death before they see the Son of man coming in his kingdom.*[13] This suggests that the kingdom is expected soon, within the lifetimes of those listening. However, he also says, in his farewell resurrection appearance (according to Matthew): *...lo, I am with you* *always, to the close of the age.*[14] The perspective here is of a distant future, when presumably the end of all things comes and God's kingdom is supreme.

Jesus frequently uses metaphors to describe what God's kingdom will be like. For example, he compares it to a heavenly feast. He sometimes makes the point that those initially invited to the feast (the Chosen People) will be excluded, while others will be invited to come instead. He says, inspired by the faith of a centurion, *I tell you, many will come from east and west and sit at table with Abraham, Isaac and Jacob in the kingdom of heaven, while the sons of the kingdom will be thrown in to the outer darkness...*[15] Similarly, on another occasion Jesus says, *The kingdom of heaven may be compared to a king who gave a marriage feast for his son, and sent his servants to call those invited to the marriage feast; but they would not come.* The king then decided to invite all and sundry to the feast: *And those servants went out into the streets and gathered all whom they found, both bad and good; so the wedding hall was filled with guests.*[16] Other metaphors, selected from many, include the harvest gathering, storing treasure in heaven and a shepherd going to find a lost sheep.[17]

The creation of a new world is also part of the expectation. In the book of Revelation the prophet says: *Then I saw a new heaven and a new earth; for the first heaven and the first earth had passed away, and the sea was no more.* And further: *He (God) will dwell with them, and they shall be his people, and God himself will be with them.* The nature of this new creation is partly expressed in negative terms: *...and death shall be no more, neither shall there be mourning nor crying nor pain any more, for the former things have passed away.*[18] This description echoes a passage in the book of Isaiah, where a similar description of *new heavens and a new earth* is expressed in equally beautiful language.[19]

What are we to make of this complex subject? Are we to expect the coming of Christ soon? Is God's kingdom round the corner? Seventh Day Adventists, who keep the Sabbath on Saturdays, originally believed that Christ was coming in 1844. When that event did not happen they still proclaimed the Second Coming, as they do today, but simply claim that it is imminent, without giving a particular date. There are Christian groups throughout the world who take a similar view and they scan the Bible, and the world around, to see if the biblical prophecies are being fulfilled. There are many such groups in the United States.

Certainly the Second Coming of Christ is a central Christian belief and this is expressed in the Christian creeds. Christ will come, it is said, *to judge both the living and the dead.* The doctrine has to be taken seriously. However, there are many mysteries associated with the Second Coming. For example, will Christ really arrive in glorious majesty, or is that description poetic? Will Christ undergo another incarnation? What will he do when he comes? Probably the best advice for Christians is that they should always be ready, that they should be watchful. After all, as Scripture says, the end of each individual may come *like a thief in the night* when death comes. Furthermore, if Christ is already with us in our day-to-day lives, then we are already part of God's kingdom. The kingdom is here: the kingdom is to come. The very last words in the Christian Bible are: *He who testifies to these things says, 'Surely I am coming soon.' Amen, come Lord Jesus. The grace of the Lord Jesus Christ be with all the saints. Amen.*[20]

NOTES

1. Joel, chapter three, verse 14.
2. Isaiah, chapter two, verse 4.
3. Ibid., chapter twenty-six, verse 21.
4. Zechariah, chapter fourteen, verse 5.
5. The word *apocalypse* is from a Greek word meaning *revelation*.
6. Mark, chapter thirteen, verses 24-27.
7. Acts, chapter one, verse 11.
8. See 1 Thessalonians, chapter four, verse 13 – chapter five, verse 2; and 2 Thessalonians, chapter two, verses 1-12.
9. See Revelation, chapters twelve and sixteen; Mark's Gospel, chapter thirteen, verse 19; Matthew's Gospel, chapter twenty-four, verse 9; 2 Thessalonians, chapter two, verse 3; and Revelation, chapters eight and nine respectively.
10. See Revelation, chapter twenty, verse 4 and 1 Corinthians, chapter fifteen, verses 23-28 respectively.
11. See *The Oxford Dictionary of the Christian Church*, *Third Edition,* eds. F.L .Cross and E.A. Livingstone, OUP, 1997, pp. 1086-7.
12. Luke, chapter seventeen, verses 20-21; and cf. Luke's Gospel, chapter eleven, verse 20.
13. Matthew, chapter sixteen, verse 28.
14. Ibid., chapter twenty-eight, verse 20.
15. Ibid., chapter eight, verses 11-12.
16. Ibid., chapter twenty-two, verses 1-14.
17. Ibid., chapter thirteen, verse 30; chapter six, verse 20; and Luke, chapter fifteen, verses 3-7 respectively.
18. Revelation, chapter twenty-one, verses 1-4.
19. Isaiah, chapter sixty-five, verses 17-25.
20. Revelation, chapter twenty-two, verses 20-21

IV
Year in, year out

This final section provides a sketch of some of the more important aspects of trying to live a Christian life. Ultimately each of us is alone before God, though some guiding principles may be useful to each and every one of us. Some such guidelines are provided in brief form. Another important aspect of the Christian life is worship and there is some consideration of what is involved in both private and public worship. In the very last chapter some problems of how to deal with the moral decisions of daily living are discussed. Biblical guidance is emphasised, but the conscience is also recognised as an important factor in decision-making.

CHAPTER THIRTEEN

Alone with eternity

While it is true that life can be so filled with work and pleasure that there is hardly a minute for anything else, sooner or later most people find such a life unsatisfying and look for something beyond that. Of course, there are other people who are educated into Christianity, or some other faith, by their parents. Yet cradle Christians sometimes have to start at square one again, because of a lack of fulfilment in their religious lives. However, there are some very fortunate people who are not only brought up as Christians, but who continue without any break and with a deepening faith. Even this last group, though, must have questions about aspects of their faith, and this must be good. Seeking the truth is part of what life is ultimately about.

How does the person searching for a faith find the right way for himself or herself? Even with Christianity there are many possible routes, and beyond Christianity there are many other faiths which can inspire a happy and fulfilling life style. Further, if someone is seeking a true way of life from a previously happy life experience, he may have different needs from someone who has had some disastrous experiences. Where does he turn when things go wrong? Another factor in the equation is temperament. What kind of religious experience is fulfilling? If a person likes a rich ceremonial, his needs will be different from someone who prefers the simple and plain without any embellishment. However, before a particular type of religion can be selected, a seeker may find it helpful to look into himself, that is, to examine his existence and his patterns of living. At the same time, he should be aware that his search might involve the proverbial chicken and egg situation. Attending a church could illuminate and inspire the personal exploration, while the personal exploration could guide a person to a particular type of church.

A sudden conversion to Christianity is always a possibility as a result of some Christian contact, or even by a direct encounter with the divine. However, many people have a more gradual experience which may last over several years, or even for a life time. The man or woman who becomes really convinced, heart and soul, that Christ is the risen Lord who is always with us, is very fortunate. This has happened to people when they are still children, and their conviction is life-long as already mentioned. It has also happened to people who are senior citizens. Age is not a consideration, except of course that the older person has more experience of life; but then he may still come to Christ as a child does, with innocence and complete trust.

Many people experience something akin to religious feeling without necessarily realising it. Awareness of beauty in a sunset or in a piece of music, awe at the extent of space beyond the stars, marvel at the intricate structure of a tiny insect, and a rich consciousness of the earth's seasons related to the seasons of human life – these are common enough experiences. Words are not needed to express what is felt on such occasions. People simply feel they are relating to some great power that they suspect may lie behind the universe. Holiness is a word often used in relation to God. Here again people can be aware of something very holy, almost fearful, in their surrounding at special times. The birth of a baby or the death of a close relative are such occasions. These events lie at the beginning and end of our conscious existence, but is there something before and after this life? Once that question is formulated in the mind, the search for God has begun.

So what is meant by a description of someone as being *religious*? Does it necessarily mean belonging to an organisation, or can a person be religious by himself? In fact, there is a sense in which religion is always a personal experience, that is, when a person is alone before God. Even in a large religious gathering, unless the religious experience is deeply personal, as well as corporate, then it can scarcely be described as a true religious experience. However, the corporate experience is very important, but having said that, it is almost certainly the case that many people have their deepest religious experiences when they are alone. There is no need to be a hermit or a dedicated mystic to have such experiences. Of course, with many religious people the solitary experience and the communal experience walk hand in hand, and the one illuminates the other. To return to the main question though – yes, it is possible to be religious without belonging to an organisation. Belief in a Supreme Being is the main criterion, but unless that belief affects the life style in some way, then it will only be a superficial form of religion. Some people start with that kind of religion and are then drawn to meet with like-minded people. This is a natural progression and it can be very enriching. However, the beliefs and practices of the group need to be assimilated in order that the convert may be truly part of that community.

Central to any religion, whether personal or communal or both, must be an attempt to relate to God. The commonest way to do this in personal religion is through prayer. But what is prayer? Contrary to what many people believe, it involves more than speaking to the unfathomable. Especially it involves more than superficially repeating the same verbal forms every day. This is not to denigrate verbal forms, for Jesus and other religious leaders have taught some very special prayers. However, if spoken prayers are used, then they need to be said thoughtfully and meaningfully – otherwise they may become pointless.

There are, in fact, many types of prayer to choose from. Painting a picture, or listening to music, or writing a poem, are examples of many possible forms of prayer. Keeping silence in the right frame of mind, and possibly in a suitable environment, is a form of prayer frequently used by church people. A suitable environment may simply be a lit candle or an icon. Some people like to be in a church to meditate in silence because they feel that the church building, its contents, and its associations, are conducive to prayer. In addition to these, there are ways of praying which do not at first seem to be prayerful. For example, going for a walk can be a form of prayer, or cleaning the house, or climbing a mountain, or helping someone who is in need. This leads to the idea that the whole of life may be sacramental. St Paul expressed this very well when he wrote: *And whatever you do, in word or deed, do everything in the name of the Lord Jesus, giving thanks to God the Father through him.* And he adds: *Whatever your task, work heartily as serving the lord, and not men...*[1] If somebody says a prayer first thing in the morning, offering the whole day and its experience to God, that is making the every day experience sacramental. Of course, the word sacrament is used in a special sense in churches and usually refers to some form of dedicated rite or ceremony. In the broad sense it may be used to dedicate all kinds of activities to God. This is relating to God: this is prayer.

Some people claim to have had very deep personal

experiences of God. Many examples of such experiences are recorded in the Bible, and many more are recorded throughout Christian history. No doubt there are also many similar experiences which have never been recorded. The man or woman living down the street may have been touched by God in some way, but never speaks of his or her experience. One wonderful example of such a special experience in the Bible is recorded by the prophet Isaiah. He seems to have been meditating alone in the temple when he had a vision of God sitting upon his throne surrounded by angels. The prophet then had a strong awareness of the holiness of God, and while he was praying *the foundations of the thresholds shook at the voice of him who called, and the house was filled with smoke.* Isaiah felt unworthy before the purity and holiness of God, but he was forgiven his sins, and then he heard a voice telling him what to do in response to God's call. The present writer never fully understood this story until he experienced the effects of a minor earthquake at which the whole house was shaken to its foundations. It is certainly claimed in the Bible that God sometimes uses natural phenomena as part of a revelation. Was it simply a coincidence that there was an earth tremor during Isaiah's vision, or was God giving him a special sign?[2]

In the New Testament, those present at Pentecost may have had a similar experience of the house shaking and trembling, though the writer compares the experience to a mighty wind. However, this experience has already been discussed above. St Paul's experience on the road to Damascus has also been mentioned, but only briefly. He was actually on his way to Damascus to persecute Christians when he was struck down by God: *...suddenly a light from heaven flashed about him. And he fell to the ground and heard a voice saying to him, 'Saul[3], Saul, why do you persecute me?'* Saul was temporarily blinded, and only regained his sight after Ananias, guided by a vision, prayed and laid hands upon him. This experience immediately changed Paul's whole life. From then on he thought of little else but taking the Gospel to the world.[4]

St Peter also had some astonishing experiences. The Transfiguration, the Day of Pentecost and his miraculous release from prison have already been mentioned above. He must have had many other deeply religious experiences, including of course, spe aking with the risen Jesus. He had another strange experience when he was told in a vision to bring about a serious change of religious policy. He was praying and meditating on the roof of the house and during a trance he *saw the heaven opened, and something descending, like a great sheet, let down by four corners on the earth. In it were all kinds of animals and reptiles and birds of the air. And there came a voice to him, 'Rise, Peter; kill and eat.'* Peter said in reply that he was not supposed to eat unclean animals, but was told that God had made them clean. After his vision Peter was visited by three messengers from a Roman centurion called Cornelius, who had been told in a vision to contact Peter. Peter went along to visit Cornelius and the upshot was that the centurion and those with him became Christians. This was the occasion of the Gentile Pentecost mentioned in an earlier chapter. Peter realised that his vision must have meant that Gentiles, who did not keep the Jewish food laws, were to come into the church. He was uplifted by this thought and said, *Truly I perceive that God shows no partiality, but in every nation anyone who fears him and does what is right is acceptable to him.*[5]

During the further course of Christian history many people have experienced visions or visitations, varying from receiving the stigmata[6] to receiving communications from angels or the Blessed Virgin Mary. Several people have received the stigmata, though St Francis is perhaps the most famous. He once changed clothes with a beggar; he embraced a leper; and he repaired ruined churches by his own labour. During a reading in church about the call of the disciples, he felt impelled to give away all he had and to devote his life to serving God. Francis, of course, founded the Franciscan Order. Another outstanding example of special experiences is that of Joan of Arc, who heard voices which were accompanied by a brilliant light. She identified some voices as those of St Michael and St Catherine and St Margaret. She was told that she had a mission to save France. Still in her teens, she led an army and was with Charles VII at his coronation. She was captured and handed over to the English. Then, after a trial, she was condemned as an heretic and burnt at Rouen. Joan of Arc is now a patron saint of France (along with St Denis). A further example is that of St Bernadette of Lourdes who saw visions of the Virgin Mary at the age of fourteen. The Virgin revealed to the girl that she (Mary) was the Immaculate Conception and a miraculous spring of water appeared at the place of the visions. The Virgin Mary commanded the building of a church at the same place. Bernadette suffered much from illness and died in a convent at the age of thirty-five. Now, of course, Lourdes is a great centre of pilgrimage and many healing miracles are associated with it.

Some people, of course, do not share such special experiences. Many Christian have never had a vision or visitation or heard angelic voices. However, what all Christians should have is a clear voice of conscience which, enlightened by the moral rules of their faith, will help them to steer a way through the difficulties of life. Those who give their lives for their faith are challenged by their consciences to witness to what they know to be the truth; and they willingly give their lives to witness to their belief in Christ as their Saviour, knowing that he will save them for the next stage of existence in immortality. The word *martyr,* in fact, is derived from a Greek word which means *witness.* The first Biblical mention of a Christian martyr tells of Stephen, an early Christian, who was able to perform many signs and wonders in the name of Jesus. He was accused of blasphemy and brought before the Jewish high priest. There Stephen gave a long address which concluded with the accusation that the Jewish hierarchy had murdered Christ. The listeners were enraged and Stephen was stoned to death, speaking of a vision of Christ in heaven as he died. There is a strange verbal irony in the description of those stoning him as witnesses (Greek *martures*). A further irony is that St Paul was also a consenting witness and, of course, he was later martyred for his faith in Christ.[7] Another early martyr was James, the brother of John. These brothers were close followers of Jesus. It was King Herod who had James killed with a sword during a persecution of Christians.[8]

Over Christian history there have been many other martyrs. One example is the martyrdom of Alban, the first recorded Christian martyr in Britain. Alban was a third-century Roman soldier who sheltered a fugitive priest. The priest converted Alban to the Christian faith, and when the priest was captured, Alban changed places with him and was executed. The city and abbey of St Alban's commemorate his name. A martyr of more recent times was Dietrich Bonhoeffer who was a Lutheran clergyman under the rule of Hitler in Germany. He had the opportunity to take a job in America at the beginning of the Second World War, but rejected the idea because he believed it was his duty to help Christians in Germany. He was forbidden to preach or publish books. In 1943 he was arrested for trying to smuggle some Jewish people into Switzerland. He was executed by the Nazis just before the end of the war at the age of thirty-nine. Despite his difficulties he left, as part of his witnessing for Christ, several books which are now world famous. Perhaps his best known book is *The Cost of Discipleship.* St Alban and Dietrich Bonhoeffer are representative of many thousands who have sacrificed their lives in the service of Christ.

Moving on to the practice of private prayer, many Christians do set aside a time for their devotions. It is appropriate at this point to explore this subject more deeply by building on what has already been said earlier in the book (see pages 32 and 38). Whatever else comes between waking in the morning and falling asleep at night, it is good to say just a few words of prayer at the beginning and end of the day. For example, when getting up someone might say simply: *This is the day which the Lord has made; let us rejoice and be glad in it.*[9] Just before going to sleep a few words of prayer might be said, such as: *I give thanks in the name of the Lord for the day that is past, and for all the wonderful things there have been in the day.* Alternatively a prayer for God's blessing might be said at either end of the day. Bearing in mind what was said above about the whole day being sacramental, nevertheless it would be good to have a short period of prayer in a more formal way. The amount of time spent is a matter of choice. It could be as short as three or five minutes, or as long as a person wishes. How should this time be used? There are endless possibilities, but some of the more popular ways of using prayer time might include using a system of Bible readings. Short readings are sensible because the reader can assimilate the meaning more meaningfully. Most Christian bookshops stock booklets with suggested Bible readings for each day. Some churches recommend a service for private evening or morning prayer but there is a lot to be said for creating one's own structure.

Common features in such structures of prayer might include: the *Lord's Prayer*, confession of sins, giving thanks for God's gifts, a prayer to show love for God and his love for us, a prayer about God's majesty and holiness; intercessions for people with various needs, a prayer for personal guidance, a prayer for one's own needs, a prayer of blessing, a prayer for the religious group to which one belongs, a prayer for the needs of the world. There are many books of prayers available in book shops, and it would not take long to put together a structure of this kind or to find a suitable one ready made.

Some people like to use key words to structure their prayer time. Here are two examples:

- ACTS stands for
    Adoration, Confession, Thanksgiving, Supplication.
- LIGHT stands for
    Love, Intercession, Guidance, Holiness, Thanksgiving.

If there is time for a period of meditation, which might include periods of silence for example, there are many books available on the subject. Some famous Christians have left systems of prayer as their heritage and often enough there are courses or retreats during which expert help is given. However, yet again, it may be that one's own structure is preferable. For example, a single basic idea could be chosen and thoughts could be arranged around this focus, with alternating silences. Take the following, which starts with the basic idea of blessing. (The stars indicate that a short silence would be appropriate.)

Each day is a blessing, Lord.
I give thanks for today and all that it may hold for me.

*

I think of all the many wonders there have been in
my life so far,
and I wait with wonder for what is to come.

*

> I thank you for the blessings of my mind and body,
> of my five senses, of the beautiful world which you
> have designed for us.
>
> *
>
> I thank you for your love which surrounds me,
> for your providence which cares for me;
> for your angels who watch over me.
>
> *
>
> Through all my times of happiness or unhappiness
> I give you thanks for your countless blessings.
>
> *
>
> For all your blessings in this life and the next,
> I praise you with all my heart and soul.

There are literally hundreds of suitable phrases in the Bible which could be used in this way. For example, to take a few random ideas, one could meditate on: the Light of the World, the Good Shepherd, the word of God, the gifts of the Holy Spirit, the armour of God, the living God, the risen Christ.

Those who wish to explore prayer and meditation more deeply should look for suitable books, or retreats to attend, or speak with a member of the clergy who will be able to give encouragement and help.

NOTES

1. Colossians, chapter three, verses 17, 23.
2. See Isaiah, chapter six.
3. St Paul changed his name from Saul while on a mission to Cyprus.
4. See Acts, chapter nine.
5. Ibid., chapter ten.
6. The marks of Christ's crucifixion on the body.
7. See Acts, chapter seven verse 1 – chapter eight, verse 1.
8. Ibid., chapter twelve, verses 1-3.
9. Psalm 118, verse 24.

CHAPTER FOURTEEN

Singing the faith

Music is a very important part of communal worship. This varies from the majestic tones of a huge organ to the strumming of guitars. Without music, worship would certainly lack a very important ingredient, though it is true that some services are held without music. These are usually of the more meditative kind.

The purpose of music during church services is to enable the congregation more worthily to express their praise of God and thanksgiving for all his gifts. In addition the story of the faith is often told in music. Hebrew psalms, translated, are frequently used and some of these may be up to three thousand years old. At the other end of the timescale there are modern hymns in today's language. Other ancient forms that are sometimes used include songs from the New Testament, for example, the words of Mary in the *Magnificat* or the words of Simeon in the *Nunc Dimittis*.[1] Such songs are sometimes called canticles. Other parts of a service which are sometimes sung include what are called versicles and responses. For example, the leader might say, *The Lord be with you* to which the response might be, *And also with you* or more traditionally, *And with your spirit.* There is great variety in the use of words and music. In some church services there may be neither traditional words nor traditional music. In other services almost everything may be traditional. In a sense it is like the difference between classical music and pop music, though these different strands are sometimes interwoven in a single act of worship.

Preparing for an act of worship is important. Music is often played before the service begins in order to set the mood. At the beginning of the actual service the leader may say a prayer with the intention of setting the right frame of mind. However, the individual may have some personal preparation that he wishes to do either before he reaches the church or just before the service. This may involve prayers or simply a time of quiet thought. What may interrupt the beginning of the service is the giving of notices or expressing a welcome to strangers. Some leaders prefer to do this at another point in the service or at the end.

If confession of sins is part of a service, this usually takes place near the beginning. This is a further stage of preparation for worshippers so that they are spiritually at ease and ready to worship God with a whole heart. There are various forms of confession. Usually the congregation repeat together a set form of words. The trouble with set forms, of course, is that they become habitual and there may be a tendency to repeat the words unthinkingly. For this reason, a short time of quietness before or after the confession is appropriate. In some churches people may also attend private confession in the presence of a priest. After the confession in a church service the priest pronounces God's forgiveness, which in some churches is called absolution. In other churches the confession and pronouncement of God's forgiveness may be much less formal.

Giving thanks to God is an important part of worship. This may be expressed incidentally in the hymns, or there may be a special thanksgiving sung or said together. On some occasions giving thanks may be more specific.

This would apply, for example, in a harvest festival. There is a very special form of thanksgiving at communion services and this is dealt with below.

In almost all forms of Christian worship, following ancient Jewish custom, there are readings from the Scriptures. Jesus himself used to attend synagogue worship and there is a story in Luke's Gospel of how he was invited to read the lesson.[2] Afterwards he gave an interpretation, which is also customary in many Christian services today. It is fairly common to have readings both from the New Testament and from the Jewish Scriptures. At communion services there is usually a reading from one of the Gospels, one from a New Testament letter, and possibly also a reading from the Jewish Scriptures. The sermon is the usual place for scriptural interpretation, though sometimes sermons are preached without any reference at all to God's word. Traditionally preachers used to begin their sermons (after an initial prayer) with a quotation from the Bible and this was intended to set the focus of his interpretation. This practice is by no means universal today. Preachers, of course, vary in their interests and in their range of skills. Sincerity and commitment can usually be spotted after two minutes of the sermon. It is fair to say that the vast majority of preachers genuinely try to preach God's word to the best of their ability. To show that it is God's word they are declaring, it is customary for many preachers to say a form of words like, *In the name of the Father, and of the Son, and of the Holy Spirit. Amen.* Some such prayer may be said both at the beginning and end of the sermon.

In many acts of worship there is an affirmation of the Christian faith. The articles of faith, as they are called, are listed in at least three creeds, two of which are commonly used. One is called the Apostles' Creed, though it was not written by the apostles. A second is called the Nicene Creed, because an early version of it was discussed at a church council at Nicaea in the fourth century AD. Both of these creeds follow a similar pattern, though the Nicene Creed is more detailed. In the first part of each creed, belief in God the Father as Creator is expressed. In the second part, belief in Jesus Christ as God's Son is expressed, together with statements about his life, death and resurrection. In the third part, belief in the Holy Spirit is expressed. Although the word Trinity is not used in these two creeds, it is obvious that God's Trinitarian nature is described. To those three parts are added articles about belief in the catholic church, the communion of saints, the forgiveness of sins, the resurrection of the body, and eternal life. A third creed is called the Athanasian Creed which is very detailed and it does mention the Trinity. It reads: *And the Catholic faith is this: That we worship one God in Trinity, and Trinity in unity.* For handy reference here is a copy of the Apostle's Creed:

I believe in God, the Father Almighty, Creator of heaven and earth.
I believe in Jesus Christ, his only Son, our Lord. He was conceived by the power of the Holy Spirit and born of the Virgin Mary. He suffered under Pontius Pilate, was crucified, died and was buried. He descended to the dead. On the third day he rose again. He ascended into heaven, and is seated at the right hand of the Father. He will come again to judge the living and the dead.
I believe in the Holy Spirit, the holy Catholic Church, the communion of saints, the forgiveness of sins, the resurrection of the body, and the life everlasting. Amen.[3]

Affirming the Commandments is another regular part of worship. Sometimes the Ten Commandments of Moses are repeated. More frequently, perhaps, the summary of the Commandments given by Jesus is read. Both of these sets of Commandments are discussed in detail in the next chapter of this book.

Intercessions or prayers are part of most church services. These may take various forms, but commonly there would be prayers for the Church, for the World, for the Community, for those in need and for the departed. The leader usually reads the prayers (or speaks extemporary prayers) and the congregation give responses, the most common of which is *Amen*, a Hebrew word which means *so be it*. Other responses might, for example, include, *And let our cry come unto you* in response to *Lord, hear our prayer*.

There are several other prayers, apart from the Lord's Prayer, which are almost universally accepted and used in worship. One, which is called the Grace, is a direct quotation from one of St Paul's letters: *The grace of our Lord Jesus Christ, and the love of God, and the fellowship of the Holy Spirit, be with us all, evermore. Amen.*[4] There are several prayers which give glory to God and one of these is called the Gloria. It is used in various ways and often at the end of a psalm. It reads: *Glory be to the Father, and to the Son, and to the Holy Spirit. Amen.* (There are several longer forms of the Gloria.) There are many blessings which are usually used at the end of a service. One of the most famous is from the Jewish Scriptures and it is called Aaron's Blessing. It says: *The Lord bless you and keep you: The Lord make his face to shine upon you, and be gracious to you: The Lord lift up his countenance upon you, and give you peace.*[5]

One of the most common words in the Bible is *peace*, Hebrew *shalom*. The Greek form is *eirene* from which the name *Irene* is derived. Jesus wished peace upon his disciples a number of times. These words, for example, are well known: *Peace I leave with you; my peace I give to you; not as the world gives do I give to you. Let not your hearts be troubled, neither let them be afraid.*[6] This idea is so important that the giving of peace is used in many church services. The leader makes a statement about peace, and then invites the congregation to exchange a sign of peace, at which people take hold each other's hands and say *The peace of the Lord be with you,* or words to that effect. Possibly this custom arises from a passage in one of St Paul's letters. He writes *...live in peace, and the God of love and peace be with you. Greet one another with a holy kiss.*[7]

Many churches remember saints or other prominent Christians on particular days of the year. These days are part of a calendar of seasons and festivals which celebrate various aspects of the Christian faith. Easter and Christmas are the obvious festivals that most people know about. Here is a very brief tabulation of the principal seasons and feast days of some of the mainstream churches:

Season or special day	Purpose of celebration
Advent (starting early December)	The coming of Christ
December 25, Christmas (and for 12 days)	The birth of Christ
Epiphany (starting 6 January)	Christ's Epiphany to the Gentiles
Sundays before Lent	Preparation for special discipline
Lent (just over six weeks before Easter)	Period of self discipline
Holy Week (the week before Easter)	The Passion of Christ
Good Friday (during Holy Week)	The Crucifixion
Easter (and for several weeks)	The Resurrection
Ascension Day	Ascension of Christ to heaven
Pentecost (Whit)	Coming of the Holy Spirit
Trinity Sunday	God is Three in One
The Trinity Season (several months)	
Sundays before Advent	Preparation for Advent
Christ the King (followed by Advent)	Christ as King in heaven

The Christian calendar tells the story of the faith, and Bible readings are usually arranged to show this. Some churches use different colours for vestments according to the day or season. It is also part of the Christian calendar to remember saints or other prominent Christians. A sample list of these is set out in chapter 11 of this book.

Many churches have flowers, candles, curtains, embroideries, carvings, stained glass windows, murals, framed pictures, carpets, altar rails and other aids to worship. Mostly these are arranged tastefully by very dedicated people and they do add an important ingredient to worship.

Perhaps the most important acts of worship in Christianity are Holy Communion and Baptism. These are called sacraments. Some churches have as many as seven sacraments, including also, marriage, ordination, penance, extreme unction (anointing when near to death) and confirmation. In medieval times the churches had many more sacraments, but over the centuries these have been reduced in number. In general, Catholic Churches practise seven sacraments, while Protestant churches use two, but there may be variations of these practices. In addition, as has already been pointed out, a person's whole life may in fact be regarded as a sacrament, if it is dedicated to God. A sacrament may be defined in a number of ways, but essentially it is an outward symbol of an inward and spiritual grace. The two main sacraments, which are biblically based, Holy Communion and Baptism, are discussed briefly below.

It is logical to discuss baptism first because it is regarded as the rite of entry into the Christian Church. This rite is mentioned frequently in the New Testament, so it obviously goes back to the earliest days of the Christian Church. Tradition claims that the institution of the sacrament even goes back to Jesus, who himself was baptised by John the Baptist. In one of his resurrection appearances Jesus is recorded as saying: *Go therefore and make disciples of all nations, baptising them in the name of the Father and of the Son and of the Holy Spirit...*[8] In biblical times whole families were baptised, so it is assumed today that it is acceptable to baptise people of any age. In some churches the person being baptised is fully immersed in water sometimes once, or sometimes three times. Just before baptism people are expected to publicly renounce Satan and all evil. In the case of babies, this is done on the baby's behalf by the parents and sponsors (godparents). In most churches a small amount of water is poured onto the person's head and the priest or minister says the traditional formula as quoted above. In some churches there is anointing with oil and a symbolic signing with a cross. Another common custom is for the baptised person to receive a lit candle, either personally, or through the parents. This is a fairly basic description of the sacrament. Different churches have other associated customs. The rite is a once for all sacrament and is not supposed to be repeated.

The sacrament of Holy Communion, sometimes called the Lord's Supper or the Mass or the Eucharist, developed directly from Jesus' last supper with his disciples when he pronounced that his body and blood are the bread and wine. The words of the institution, as they are called, are given in slightly different forms in the synoptic Gospels[9] and Paul's first letter to Corinth. These are usually conflated into one form. The oldest of the records is most likely Paul's account. He writes: *For I received from the Lord what I also delivered to you, that the Lord Jesus on the night when he was betrayed took bread, and when he had given thanks, he broke it, and said, 'This is my body which is for you. Do this in remembrance of me.' In the same way also the cup, after supper, saying, 'This cup is the new covenant in my blood. Do this as often as you drink it, in remembrance of me.' For as often as you eat this bread and drink this cup, you proclaim the Lord's death until he comes.*[10] Because Jesus gave thanks, the church service is often called the *Eucharist* which comes from the Greek word for thanks. For the same reason, the central part of the communion service is often called the Prayer of Thanksgiving. During this prayer the priest blesses the bread and wine on the altar or table and repeats the words of Jesus at the Last Supper.

There are various ways of distributing the bread and wine in different churches, just as there are various words which are said to the recipient. One of the shortest forms is for the minister or priest to say, *The body of Christ,* as he or she gives someone a piece of bread; and, *The blood of Christ,* as wine is given. As to the purpose of the rite, the name *Communion* shows that the believers who take part are in communion (or fellowship) with Christ and with each other. In general, Roman Catholic churches emphasise the sacrifice of the mass while the Protestant churches emphasis the idea of a memorial. Some churches, including the Catholic churches believe that there is a change in the bread and wine and that the elements actually become the body and blood of Christ. Other churches believe the bread and wine remain the same, though Christ is present spiritually. The whole issue of Communion is very complicated and associated issues are often disputed. What is said here is a simple introduction.

Choosing which church to attend may present problems. Anyone thinking of joining a church would do well to explore the different possibilities in the area where they live and to find out something about the practices of each church. In the end it may be a matter of temperament. Some people, for example, feel at home with a lot of ceremonial, and priests that wear vestments.

Others may feel at home in a simple chapel where the ornaments may be restricted to a few flowers and where the minister wears normal everyday clothes. There are numerous factors to take into account, including the sort of welcome strangers are given. It is probably a good idea to attend occasional services in several different churches before choosing one as a spiritual home.

NOTES

1. See Luke, chapter one, verses 46-55; and chapter two, verses 29-32.
2. Ibid., chapter four, verses 16-30.
3. Quoted from *The Alternative Service Book 1880*, CUP et al., p. 80.
4. 2 Corinthians, chapter thirteen, verse 14.
5. Numbers, chapter six, verses 24-6.
6. John, chapter fourteen, verse 27.
7. 2 Corinthians, chapter thirteen, verses 11-12.
8. Matthew, chapter twenty-eight, verse 19.
9. Ibid., chapter twenty-six, verses 26-29; Mark, chapter fourteen, verses 22-25; and Luke, chapter twenty-two, verses 14-23.
10. 1 Corinthians, chapter eleven, verses 23-26.

CHAPTER FIFTEEN

Map reading

Navigating through life may sometimes be very difficult. This is true for every human being. Problems arise and solutions need to be found. Christianity, however, does offer a number of aids to navigation. One of the most important of these is a system of moral guidelines – in practice, Christian ethics. Of course, other religions have their ethical systems and there is remarkable similarity between the rules given by most of the higher religions.

It is also true that there are systems of ethics which have nothing to do with religion and these are often useful. For example, to make a decision on the basis of what is best for the greatest number of people may be a good way to solve a problem. However, some Christian rules have been filtered into common parlance. A good example of this is the frequently used phrase, *love your neighbour*. While this shows that moral systems have common features, one of the main troubles today is that some people do not like rules and make up their own morality on the hoof. This usually means that what suits them is right.

Christianity, on the other hand, offers timeless rules. Even so, each generation has to learn how to apply these rules in new situations. It is perhaps better to think of the Ten Commandments, for example, as moral principles which guide our thinking, and not as laws set in concrete.

As explained below, Jesus summarised the Ten Commandments (and many others) in two rules which emphasise love for God and love for other people. In effect, Christian ethics is the human response to God's love.

The Ten Commandments are respected by Jewish people, as well as by Christians. Two copies of the Commandments are to be found in the Jewish Scriptures.[1] A reading of these shows that the first four are about relating to God and the remaining six are about relating to people. When Jesus summarised the law he made a similar division. He said, *The first (law) is, 'Hear, O Israel: The Lord our God, the Lord is one; and you shall love the Lord your God with all your heart, and with all your soul, and with all your mind, and with all your strength.' The second is this, 'You shall love your neighbour as yourself.'*[2] It is often forgotten that both of these laws appeared first in the Jewish Scriptures. Jesus, in fact, selected these two laws from a large collection of legal material to show us the crux of true morality.[3]

The ethical commandments of the Decalogue (Ten Laws) may be summarised as follows:

> Honour your parents.
> Do not kill.
> Do not commit adultery.
> Do not steal.
> Do not bear false witness.
> Do not covet.

These were originally designed for a closed community living in the desert. However, all of these laws appeared in one form or another in other civilisations which existed before Moses, who produced the Decalogue. Breaking any of these rules causes trouble and unhappiness. Nevertheless, there are times when it may be right to break one of the Commandments. For example, if a woman is deserted by her husband for another woman, it would be understandable if she found another partner, though in a strict religious sense she would be committing adultery. Yet again, if a woman has three children and no income at all for whatever reason, most people would feel she would be justified in stealing food for the children, though of course she would still be stealing. These examples are pointers to what often happens in life, that is, when people have to choose the lesser of two evils.

Jesus comments on these Jewish laws, especially in his famous Sermon on the Mount.[4] Of the law forbidding killing he says, ... *everyone who is angry with his brother is liable to judgement...* Of the law forbidding adultery he says, ...*everyone who looks at a woman lustfully has already committed adultery in his heart...* Of the law on swearing falsely he says, *Let what you say be simply 'Yes' or 'No'; anything more than this comes from evil.*[5] A moment's thought will show that Jesus is not throwing out these Commandments, but making them more demanding by piercing to the root of the sins involved.

Jesus is even more demanding when he comments on the law about loving one's neighbour. He says, *Love your enemies and pray for those who persecute you.*[6] Further there is a law in the Jewish Scriptures which demands an eye for an eye and a tooth for a tooth.[7] On this subject Jesus says, *But if anyone strikes you on the right cheek, turn to him the other also...*[8] As anyone knows who has tried to follow this rule, it is extremely difficult to achieve. In fact, in medieval times it was believed that the Sermon on the Mount was for the great saints to follow, and that the ordinary Christian could not hope to keep to it.

Both the Jewish Scriptures and the New Testament make clear that the heart of ethics consists of care and love for other people. The prophet Isaiah, for example, writes, *...cease to do evil, learn to do good; seek justice, correct oppression; defend the fatherless, plead for the widow.*[9] In a similar way, a psalmist prays for the king: *May he defend the cause of the poor of the people, give deliverance to the needy, and crush the oppressor.*[10] In the New Testament there are many similar examples. Jesus says, *...for I was hungry and you gave me food, I was thirsty and you gave me drink, I was a stranger and you welcomed me, I was naked and you clothed me, I was sick and you visited me, I was in prison and you came to me.*[11] One of the most famous parables of Jesus, which he told to illustrate what it means to love one's neighbour, is the story of the Good Samaritan. Many people know the story, but just as a reminder, it is about a man who was mugged and robbed. He was left lying in the road. A Jewish priest came along and walked past, as did a temple official. But then a despised Samaritan came along and he gave the injured man first aid and took him to an inn where he paid for the victim to stay. It was obviously the Samaritan who loved his neighbour.[12]

Loving one's neighbour includes the idea of service on behalf of other people. To illustrate this point Jesus carries out a parable in action by washing the feet of his disciples. This piece of teaching took place at the Last Supper.[13]

The Christian ethic includes forgiveness, as in the Lord's Prayer which states, *Forgive us our trespasses, as we forgive those who trespass against us.* In addition, Jesus emphasises that we should not judge our neighbours. In the Sermon on the Mount he says in a timeless parable, *Judge not, that you be not judged. For with the judgement you pronounce you will be judged, and the measure you give will be the measure you get. Why do you see the speck that is in your brother's eye, but do not notice the log that is in your own eye?*[14]

At the same time, Jesus argues that evil thoughts lead to evil actions. *What comes out of a man is what defiles a man. For from within, out of the heart of man, come evil thoughts, fornication, theft, murder, adultery, coveting, wickedness, deceit, licentiousness, envy, slander, pride, foolishness. All these evil things come from within, and they defile a man.*[15] Here again Jesus strikes to the crux of morality and reinforces the Mosaic Commandments.

Strategies for answering moral questions

Do Christians need to look elsewhere apart from the Bible for guidance on moral questions? Or is it essential to know about all the many and varied theories of ethics which abound? In general the guidance of the Bible and familiarity with general Christian teaching should be sufficient for most of us.

Given that God is our Creator and that he has revealed himself to us, what ought to be our goal in our decision making? Whatever people's actions are, surely they ought to be directed to the building of God's kingdom. If God has revealed the nature of his love, then human beings need to try to imitate this love. The kingdom of heaven is a community of love, and in any community some basic rules are essential.

In ethical terms, this is what the biblical revelation provides, as already noted. People often concentrate either on Jesus' summary of the law or on the Ten Commandments. To be sure, these are useful first steps. However, the more people know about the complexities of biblical ethics, the more likely they are to be prepared for the complex decisions that life often puts before them. A knowledge of human nature is also extremely useful.

Starting out then with a reasonable knowledge of the Bible and a reasonable knowledge of human nature, we should have a good basis for making decisions. Yet, even so, there are various strategies that may be used. Then, in addition, there is the matter of temperament. If a person likes sticking to rules he may use different strategies from someone who makes decisions on a more emotional basis.

If a person feels comfortable with keeping to rules, then probably the ethical negatives will be attractive. It seems easier, somehow, to have many of the answers decided beforehand by an authoritative statement such as the Ten Commandments. Part of the time the system could work very well. However, every now and again a conflict of interests might appear. Suppose, for example, somebody notices that a colleague and friend is stealing money from the petty cash and is succeeding in concealing the thefts. To pretend not to notice amounts to cheating the employer and being party to the theft. But here is a conflict between obeying the rules and being loyal to a friend. Possibly some compromise answer to the problem may be found, such as having a quiet word with the friend and agreeing with him that the money should be quietly repaid. This simple example illustrates that keeping to the rules is not always easy.

Of course, people may use positive rules as well as negative ones. For example, a person could decide to give something to every charity which contacts him or to every beggar he meets in the street. He might also decide to spend a regular time each week reading to blind people.

On the other hand, some people are uncomfortable with rules. Some people might like to decide all issues on the basis of Christian love. Certainly it can be argued, that the New Testament would support such an approach to some extent (see Matthew 22:34-40). Unfortunately, it is not always easy to perceive what the correct loving action ought to be.

Sometimes it is necessary to decide which is the lesser of two evils. In order to do this it is necessary to weigh up the pros and cons of every possible action. In fact, people are quite often placed in a position where it is difficult to avoid hurting someone, whatever action is taken. This is where the principle of the lesser of two evils may be brought into play. Take the use of the atomic bomb which ended the Second World War between the Allies and Japan. It is often argued that the dropping of two very powerful bombs on Hiroshima and Nagasaki ended the war immediately, so saving many lives. So to drop the bombs was the lesser of two evils. However, if a longer view is taken, then the dropping of those bombs could have been considered as creating a precedent for a future war. Therefore, if another major world war should take place, then even more powerful bombs could mean the destruction of the whole planet. On that basis, it could be argued that the lesser of two evils was not to use the atomic bombs in 1945, but to continue the war with conventional weapons.

"What is best for the majority?" is another useful question. This is one of the principles of a system called utilitarianism, that is, to bring about the greatest good for the greatest number of people. The previous paragraph, in fact, has demonstrated this idea. Another example might be the case of a man with limited provisions for a large number of starving people. If he gives everyone a small share they will all die anyway. However, if he gives smaller number of people something to eat, people with skills which would be helpful to the community in the future, then he could defend his decision by arguing that ultimately more people would benefit because the community could grow again and have descendants. Otherwise the whole community would disappear.

The conscience sometimes makes its own demands, which are difficult to ignore. The man in the previous example might be prompted by his conscience to feed all the people at whatever cost, because his conscience would not allow him to condemn some people to death. There is also what we call a gut feeling which is not at the rational level, whereas the conscience usually is. Intuition is possibly somewhere between the two. At any rate, emotional reaction and/or an inner moral command are often influential in decision making.

The Christian normally wishes to lead his life according to God's will. In some circumstances there is little difficulty in knowing what the divine will would be. For example, if a man had a sudden impulse to steal an expensive second-hand book of great historical value from the university library, even though he believes he could get away with it, his moral training would inhibit him from actually stealing the book. He may or may not consciously think about God's will when suppressing the impulse, but if he were asked, he would assert strongly that stealing is against the will of God. Of course, it is not always easy to decide what God's will is and sometimes a clear-cut decision cannot be made without considerable thought.

The use of an imaginary devil's (or angel's) advocate is a useful strategy. The devil's arguments could be listed in one column and the angels' arguments alongside in another column. For example, if a man and his wife were trying to decide whether to adopt a child for compassionate reasons, they might have some doubts because they already have four children. The devil's advocate might argue that the existing children would suffer, that finances would be over stretched, that the adopted child might disrupt family life and that it might be in the child's best interests to wait for adoptive parents without so many existing commitments. On the other hand, the angel's advocate might argue that the love already within the family would carry the adopted child, that somehow they would manage financially by cutting down on unnecessary luxuries, that it would be good for their own children to learn to adapt and to show compassion – and so on. Once all the arguments had been considered, then a decision could be taken.

There are some difficulties in Bible based ethics, for while the ethical principles which the Bible gives are good guidelines, each person has to work out for himself appropriate solutions to the problems he or she faces. Furthermore, the practical examples given in biblical stories may not be exact parallels for today's problems. The individual responsibility God has given to each person is also a vital factor. Each of us needs to face up to the moral challenges life puts us.

Christian groups often express views on moral issues. This does not remove the individual's responsibility for thinking out his own position. After careful thought, he may not agree with every aspect of what the group advises, in which case it may be necessary to make a stand on the grounds of conscience.

In all ethical judgements the Christian will not only take biblical principles into account, but he will surely pray for guidance in making his decision. He may not receive a phone call from heaven, but the Holy Spirit will work within him to find the right way forward.

NOTES

1 Exodus, chapter twenty; and Deuteronomy, chapter five.
2 Mark, chapter twelve, verses 29-31.
3 See Deuteronomy, chapter six, verses 4-5; Leviticus, chapter nineteen, verses, 18, 34.
4 Matthew, chapters 5-7.
5 Ibid., chapter five, verses 22, 28, 37, respectively.
6 Ibid., verse 44.
7 Known as the *lex talionis*.

8 Ibid., verse 39.
9 Isaiah, chapter one, verses 16-17.
10 Psalm 72, verse 4.
11 Matthew, chapter twenty-five, verses 35-36.
12 Luke, chapter ten, verses 25-37.
13 John, chapter thirteen, 2-20.
14 Matthew, chapter seven, 1-3.
15 Mark, chapter seven, verses 20-23.